VICENTE WOLF

Creative Interior Solutions

VICENTE WOLF

Creative Interior Solutions

Text by
Margaret Russell

Foreword by
Marianne Williamson

RIZZOLI
NEW YORK

New York · Paris · London · Milan

Contents

Foreword

In 1992 I published a book called *A Return to Love*. Never having published before, my prayer was simply that it would sell enough copies that I wouldn't be embarrassed.

The book was fated for much more, as Oprah Winfrey announced on *The Oprah Winfrey Show* that it was the best book she had ever read.

On that day, as you can imagine, my life changed.

As the book soared to the top of the bestseller lists, one of the first calls I received was from my mother. She said simply, "Promise me you will buy a new bed."

I laughed. "You don't like the black Formica headboard with the colored lights?"

"No, I do not," said my mother. "Now go buy a new bed."

I asked my literary agent, "Do you think I can afford a new bed?" He laughed and said, "Several."

And so, I did as I was told.

Shopping for a piece of furniture thinking only about what I found beautiful was a new experience for me. Accompanied by a decorator friend, I visited a store in Los Angeles.

And there I saw it. "That's the most beautiful bed I've ever seen," I said to my friend. It was a tufted sleigh bed with lines that were so stunning I felt like I was looking at a piece of art.

"That's a Vicente Wolf," she said. And that was it. I was in love.

I loved that bed so much that I had a habit of looking at it, stroking the headboard, and saying, "Ah, my Vicente Wolf."

One night, a man who had been sleeping in that bed for several months sat up straight, looked me in the eye, and said, "I just have to say, I don't know who this Vicente Wolf character is, but I'm here now."

Once I explained the situation to him, we both laughed heartily, and we still laugh about it now. "We'll always have Vicente Wolf!"

Years later, Vicente Wolf was seated next to me at a book fair, and I was starstruck. "You're *the* Vicente Wolf?" I exclaimed. I didn't have time to explain how much a part of my life he had become, but I did tell him I was his biggest fan.

Several years after that, I saw Vicente give a presentation about interior design and I thought, if one bed is that beautiful, just imagine what a whole room designed by him would be like. From there, I moved on to imagining what he could do with a whole apartment, and then to making the vision come true: I asked Vicente to design an apartment in New York for me.

When the day of the installation arrived, I was told I had to leave and not come back until Vicente and a colleague had put everything in place. After they finished, I walked in and was amazed. It was as though I had entered a completely different apartment. The new space was one of beauty and rest and uplift—beyond anything I could have imagined or created for myself. I looked at Vicente with tears in my eyes as I said, "Thank you, Vicente. Thank you."

Beauty matters. The energy in our homes matters. Line and proportion matter. Design matters. They affect feelings and clarity of thought, and even depth of insight. It is an honor to live in an apartment designed by the great Vicente Wolf. As someone who travels for work as much as I do, coming home to an environment that nurtures and nourishes me has been one of my greatest pleasures. Talent such as Vicente's is rare, and to this day I'm grateful that my mother made me buy that bed.

—Marianne Williamson

OPPOSITE: When Marianne asked me to design her Manhattan apartment, I knew it had to be glamorous. Because she had a lovely Chinese cocktail table and dark floors, I used an iridescent black wallpaper and reupholstered her furniture in a bold palette of black and white.

Introduction

The path that led to my life as an interior designer started in Havana, where I was born and lived with my family until 1961, when my parents and I left Cuba for America; I was 15 years old. My childhood was spent in a design-focused world, as my mother and father ran a successful construction-related business and would regularly bring me to building sites and architect meetings. School was a constant struggle; we didn't know at the time that I am severely dyslexic. I was extremely visual, however, and fascinated by the color and composition, light and shadow that surrounded me. Though I have never returned to Cuba, the memories of that time remain firmly etched in my mind.

After the revolution, we left our prosperous life in Havana and arrived in Miami Beach as political refugees. This was a profoundly difficult time for my family—my parents eventually divorced, and I dropped out of school. When I turned 18, I followed my dreams to New York City.

With limited education and no real career plan, I dabbled in everything from advertising and fashion merchandising to modeling and acting, though to no great success. Then, in my mid-20s, I met Bob Patino, the manager of a design showroom. His work intrigued me, and I took a job sweeping floors in a similar showroom; soon I was working directly with designers when they shopped. Not long after, Bob and I became both business and personal partners, launching Patino/Wolf Associates in 1974.

He was the extrovert, and I was the introvert—while he was socializing to attract new clients, I quietly worked on our interiors projects, studying and educating myself along the way; I am a complete autodidact. The firm flourished as we received accolades for our modern, streamlined aesthetic and surprisingly glamorous use of industrial materials. In the summer of 1986, Bob had a catastrophic car accident, and he took over a year to recover while I assumed responsibility for our company, gaining new clients to sustain our success. When he returned, everything had changed, and our personal and business relationships came to a crashing halt. We had built a business together for nearly 15 years, but I left with nothing.

In October of 1988, I started my new life with one loyal client, a $5,000 nest egg, and a live/work loft in a seedy part of town. My survivor mentality kicked in, and though my first move was recouping projects Patino/Wolf had recently rejected, I gained new clients as I found my own voice.

Travel to far-flung destinations like India, Nepal, Papua New Guinea, Madagascar, Borneo, and Laos informed my eye and influenced my point of view; it does to this day. And though the Patino/Wolf world had been strictly structured—staff dressed in black or white or a combination thereof—I eagerly embraced a looser attitude. I confidently navigated the dueling design dialogues of 1980s "Bonfire of the Vanities" excess and high-tech minimalism, building a portfolio of design work with a distinctive aesthetic. My interiors were still clean, but softer, and with an earthy warmth.

Six months after my split with Bob, my loft was showcased in a four-page spread in *The New York Times Magazine*. I'm appreciative that I was in the right place at the right time and have never looked back.

I've always worked hard because I love what I do and don't consider it work—and it's a pleasure to be surrounded by people who are equally passionate. Over the years, I've been fortunate to collaborate with a diverse team of talented creatives, both within my office and at our project worksites; they continually inspire me. Our work now comprises residential and commercial projects around the world, with a core of long-standing clients who regularly offer fresh opportunities, as well as the wonderful kismet of brand-new clients who bring their exciting challenges.

Generous mentors have helped to guide my life not only as a collector but also as a photographer. And my career has been deeply influenced by other designers—especially the work of legendary British decorator David Hicks, who transformed traditional interiors into contemporary homes for modern lives. Though I never met David Hicks, he taught me, and I believe it's important to share what I've learned as others have shared with me. This is why I like to teach—and to publish books such as this one, with the hope that it may inspire you on your creative path.

OPPOSITE: A serene setting became the cover of the December/January 1995 issue of *Elle Decor*, one of my most memorable magazine cover stories. The canopied daybed and slipcovered chairs are dressed in yards and yards of a pale gray-blue Manuel Canovas fabric.

CLOCKWISE, FROM ABOVE: My former partner, Bob Patino, with me in a Patino/Wolf–designed project. A model room that we designed for a 1980s Zeckendorf building, with black tiled floors and an Irving Penn photograph. The bed in a late 1970s bedroom was set into a carpeted built-in platform, which was surprisingly popular at the time. OPPOSITE: The living room of a New Jersey house featured soaring ceilings and a peaked skylit roof; Bob and I collaborated on the interiors, but this was my first architectural-design project.

THE NEW

WHITE

ROOM

The new white room may indeed have stark white walls, lacquered white floors and spare furnishings, but the space is neither antiseptic nor forbidding. "In today's white room, objects no longer have to be modern and only white, nor do the structural underpinnings have to be concealed," says Vicente Wolf, formerly of Patino/Wolf and now head of his own design firm. To illustrate this theory, he used his Manhattan loft, shown here, and juxtaposed gilt antique furniture and exposed radiators, placed a muted Aubusson rug underneath bare pipes and hung diaphanous silk curtains against industrial windows.

"Old rules that had long been governing my work were put aside," recalls Vicente Wolf, referring to the design of his white rooms. "It no longer mattered whether the upholstery matched or if everything was contemporary. I wanted the feeling to be more relaxed, more human and livable." As a result, he mixed old and new furnishings. Some pieces, such as a number of high-tech black lamps, were only just recently retrieved from storage. Yet the atmosphere has glamour, in part because of the way antiques are used as if they were sculpture floating in space. "I became especially enamored of antique chairs," he says. "Each has a different personality, and I like to watch visitors pick the one that suits them best." ■

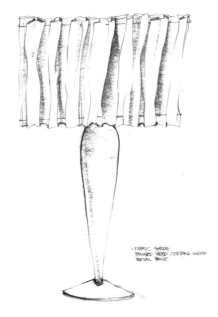

· FABRIC SHADE
STAINED WOOD / ZEBRA WOOD
METAL BASE

OPPOSITE: A model room for a Zeckendorf building that was one of my first projects on my own; I used three design elements that have remained signatures throughout my career: a sumptuous upholstered wall, a sculptural sleigh bed, and a dramatic overscale wall mirror. **ABOVE, CLOCKWISE FROM TOP LEFT:** Editorial coverage has been essential to my success, and this four-page spread in an April 1989 issue of *The New York Times Magazine* boldly launched my solo career barely six months after Patino/Wolf split up. The *Times* photographed my loft, which you can see as it is today starting on page 232. A May 1991 cover story in *Metropolitan Home* featured my room design for that year's Kips Bay Decorator Show House, my first of many show-house projects. Product design is a great passion of mine and over the years I have created collections with a wide range of manufacturing partners, including furniture for Ralph Pucci, Henredon, Carsons, and Casa Bique; Sasaki tableware; Kravet fabrics; paints for PPG; crystal accessories for Baccarat and Steuben; rugs for Tufenkian and Doris Leslie Blau; tiles for Ann Sacks; and a webbed furniture line for Niedermaier that is now sold at VW Home. I've always been particularly focused on lighting in my interiors, and have designed collections for a variety of companies, including Paul Hanson, for whom we produced this high-contrast showroom display. The living room of a Jackson Hole, Wyoming, log cabin that I designed in the early 1990s offered an unexpected take on mountain style; I recently spent a weekend at the house and was thrilled to see that the decor still looks as fresh today as it did then. A sketch for one of my lamps for Paul Hanson that was inspired by the Vienna Secession movement of the late 19th century.

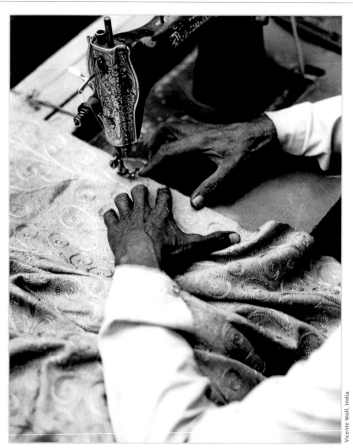

ABOVE, CLOCKWISE FROM TOP LEFT: Windows stainless-steel flatware, one of several patterns that I created for Sasaki, was inspired by the work of Scottish architect Charles Rennie Mackintosh. I also designed several Sasaki dinnerware collections, including this one influenced by tribal motifs. Anichini, the luxury linen company, commissioned me to photograph a series of advertisements for them, which I shot in black-and-white film while traveling to far-flung locales. I would pack a few samples of their bedding or towels and shoot them in exotic settings; this image was taken on a trip to India. As a long-time admirer of Baccarat crystal, I was excited when asked to design a line of accessories for the company, including a stacked candleholder and various vases. I designed this sterling-silver flatware, inspired by a Flemish still-life painting, that we sold at VW Home. OPPOSITE, CLOCKWISE FROM TOP LEFT: In addition to my residential work, I've designed several restaurants in cities located around the world, including L'Impero, which opened in Manhattan in 2002. In the living room of a client's beach cottage, I mounted a marvelous collection of plaster Beaux-Arts architectural molds to fill an entire wall. Though I'm not known for vibrant interiors, when I use a bright color, I go all the way, as in Diego, a Mexican restaurant I designed at the MGM Grand in Las Vegas. In 1991, my landlord asked if I was interested when the loft space adjacent to my office became available. I didn't need more room but jumped at the chance to open a design shop, promptly buying plane tickets for a shopping trip that took me literally around the world. Since then, VW Home has catered to both consumers and the design trade, offering a mix of antique and vintage pieces, some textiles, and signature furniture and objects that I design and have made.

Design Evolutions

Throughout my career I have never taken lightly the responsibility to help clients transform an apartment or a house into a well-designed home—a place where they will not only live but also entertain family and friends and perhaps raise their children. More than four walls and furniture, a home is the very foundation of their lives.

Occasionally, new clients hire me to redesign a current residence because of a recent life change, and I'm often asked to rethink a previous project for clients who become empty nesters. Though emotions can run so strong that I feel like a combination designer-therapist, it's proof that interior design is more than a superficial art—it's a necessity.

Space to Breathe

A few years ago, a wonderful couple who are longtime clients and dear friends came to me and requested something that, perhaps surprisingly, I had never been asked to do before: They wanted me to reimagine part of a project I had designed for them previously—not merely an update, but a sweeping style shift.

We had worked together several times, and nearly two decades earlier I designed a Manhattan apartment for them in a gracious prewar building on Fifth Avenue, one of the finest in Carnegie Hill. It was a spacious family home with treetop views, one they envisioned in an elegant, traditional style, filled with fine antiques, sumptuous damask upholstery, and their striking collection of art. My frequent attempts to propose something a bit less staid, perhaps a wonderful raffia carpet, were to no avail; the husband opted instead for an intricate Tabriz I found at Doris Leslie Blau. It ended up being a lovely project—decorated in a style I would describe as "serious"—and a reflection of their taste and very social lifestyle at the time. To be honest, they are a delightful, youthful couple with a great sense of humor, and I always considered this home to be far more serious than they were!

Fast-forward several years, when my clients realized that they were craving a streamlined, less formal way of life. With no intention of moving to a new apartment, they instead asked if I could create a fresh, younger, lighter look while employing as many as possible of their existing furnishings. I was thrilled by the prospect, as I could now actually create the home I had always imagined for my friends and their family. Repurposing current pieces was of little concern; after all, I had purchased most of them. As it turned out, the changes we made weren't at all severe or drastic—my clients trusted me not to propel them from 18th century to disco—and I completely transformed their public rooms to reflect their new mindset and simplified lifestyle.

The living room's architecture remained untouched, but we reinvigorated the room's envelope by removing the patterned rug and bleaching the dark floors. The new plush carpet is symmetrical and strict, delineated by a bold woven grid that provides a strong yet subtle foundation to the more modern quality of the space. I painted the dusky off-white walls a crisp PPG color called Delicate White, and we kept the existing ceiling fixture, which is a wonderful contemporary piece I found in Paris. I'll admit that it had always looked a bit out of place in its former traditional setting, but it became one of the key elements of the new space—elements which all spoke the same language.

The carved-marble fireplace mantel was replaced with one I designed in a combination

OPPOSITE: I conceived of the steel mantel to serve as a focal point, with its combination of matte and shiny surfaces designed to reflect and refract views of the room. The Joan Miró aquatint is hung off-center, next to an antique Roman torso, and vintage crystal sconces produce a soft glow.

of satin and polished steel. Now the focal point of the room, it offers glints and glances of the space reflected on its multilevel planes. Vintage Murano-glass sconces studded with jewel-like crystal spheres punctuate the wall above, serving as a poetic counterpoint to the mantel's sleek lines.

This is a spacious room, one that stretches over 30 feet long and 18 feet wide, and I was able to utilize nearly 60 percent of my clients' furniture in my reconfigured floor plan, relocating the pieces within the space and creating a new sense of balance and calm. To showcase the views of Central Park, I replaced the silk window coverings with translucent linen shades that filter the sunlight on even the brightest of days, and the damask-covered sofa and armchairs were reupholstered in cloud-white fabrics—though with rambunctious grandchildren in mind, I selected easy-care, soil-resistant performance textiles. I transformed some of the existing dark wood furniture with white paint in a semigloss finish, including a pair of overscale mirrors that flank the entrance. What was once dark is now light.

Midcentury-modern classics were mixed with the clients' antiques, which include an exquisite gilded console; a tufted white leather Mies van der Rohe daybed now sets the tone as you enter, and a pair of sculptural Warren Platner chairs softens the room's linear axes. The original layout featured a tall folding screen that I had placed as an architectural foil to break up the long sofa wall—formerly upholstered in a silk with a subtle sheen, the screen is now clad in a crisp white canvas and sits behind the daybed, just inside the entrance.

The final step was rehanging my clients' art, which was an important element in both the old and new spaces. I moved *Irises*, a moody Robert Mapplethorpe black-and-white image, from its position centered over the sofa to hang above a long console table closer to the windows; a small 1920s platinum photograph of waterlilies, in an elaborate golden frame, is now displayed quite low and off-balance just over a corner of the sofa. It is a quirky placement that prompts one to focus on it. I determined that hanging three Richard Serra etchings vertically over the gilded console—they were previously displayed in the foyer—would add a pleasing height and balance to the space. A wall sculpture by Pard Morrison is installed behind the piano, at the far end of the room; a small marble Roman torso is placed beside a Joan Miró aquatint above the mantel; and a work by Conrad Marca-Relli hangs over the daybed, near a group of 18th-century Italian altar candleholders that I found in the Paris flea market.

Revealing a newly installed project is always exciting, and when my clients first saw their new living room, the husband was particularly amazed that so many pieces that they treasured somehow looked completely different in this space—once so familiar—that now felt bigger, brighter, and more modern. The wife, who perhaps might have always leaned a tad more contemporary than classic, flashed me a happy smile as she exclaimed, "Ah! Now I can really breathe."

LEFT: The overall feeling of the living room was freshened and brightened through liberal use of the color white—I used bright-white paint to coat the walls and some furniture pieces; the window shades and upholstery fabrics are white; and the striking carpet, which was woven of wool, silk, and viscose in a raised grid pattern, provides soothing tones of white underfoot. All that was formal and dark—floors and furniture—is now light.

Design Lessons

° My clients were both surprised and pleased when I told them I would repurpose several existing pieces in the new iteration of this project—I think they feared I would want to start from scratch! When redoing a space, don't feel that you must discard everything—look at the pieces you love most, that give you pleasure, and either update them or use them in a different way.

° If there are several traditional-style pieces in a space, think about adding a few modern classics that might make the stodgier pieces feel more contemporary— remember, all things were contemporary at one time.

° In a space with classic architectural detail, I like to paint the ceiling, walls, and moldings in the same color; they still stand out, but they feel less formal.

° I love using folding screens to add interest and a play of light to a room that might otherwise feel boxy. They offer the opportunity to hang something on them, and if they are upholstered, they can bring an unexpected sense of softness to a space.

° Using a geometric pattern on a floor or a carpet gives you the freedom to have irregular shapes in a space, as well as an unexpected flow or floor plan. For instance, the grid carpet in this apartment offered a wonderful foundation for a less rigid furniture arrangement—furniture should never hug all four walls of a room.

OPPOSITE, FAR LEFT: I moved the Robert Mapplethorpe photo-graph from its center placement over the sofa and grouped it with a 1950s marble lamp from France and a magical gilded peacock that I found in Burma. A pair of club chairs were removed in favor of Warren Platner's lounge chairs for Knoll, which now flank the sofa; their sculptural lines soften the geometry of the seating area. NEAR LEFT: Instead of replacing the original damask-covered sofa, which featured a rounded back that now looked dated, I straightened its lines and reupholstered it in a bright-white performance fabric by Janus et Cie. And though I switched the earth-toned Tabriz rug with one custom made by Stark in a textured grid pattern, we kept the X-base cocktail table. RIGHT: The marble-topped gilded console is 18th-century French, and the etchings from Richard Serra's "Venice Notebook" series were previously displayed horizontally in the foyer, though I prefer them here, where they have stronger impact hung vertically. They add a sense of height and balance to the space.

LEFT: Knoll's iconic Barcelona couch by Mies van der Rohe is set perpendicular to a monumental folding screen, which was previously placed near the center of the room to serve as an architectural foil. The artwork is by Conrad Marca-Relli, the floor lamp is a Serge Mouille design, and the tripod table is a Cedric Hartman classic; I found the French 1940s armchair to replace a more formal antique Swedish chair. The gilded 18th-century Italian candleholders are from the Paris flea market.

A Fresh Start

Prospective clients often come to me after experiencing major shifts in their lives, wanting their homes to reflect their new situations and mindsets. My initial response is always a warning to be prepared not only to let go of much of their furniture, but also to discard preconceived ideas and design misconceptions. And letting go is never easy.

The circumstances regarding this Manhattan apartment were particularly sensitive. My clients were a recently married couple, and the husband, who is involved in the entertainment industry, lived here for many years with his first wife, who had passed away. Though he was embracing a new life with a vibrant new partner, he had no interest in moving to a new home. His wife, who had followed my work for some time and even referred friends to me, though we had not yet met, was sure I could help them find a solution: My challenge was to reinvent the existing space to reflect their shared lives.

To be honest, when I first walked into the apartment, my heart sank. The living room decor was very traditional, very French, with elaborate millwork and applied moldings, an ornate marble fireplace with ormolu mounts, and lively patterned upholstery and rugs; pelmets and flowing curtains were installed at each window. The ceilings were high but looked weighted down by the layers of detail below, and though the room was thoughtfully put together, it felt as if it were from another time. Creating a fresh look and experience for my clients would require far more than a minor facelift.

Patience was needed on all sides as I worked with my clients to visualize what their new home might be. A palette of soft, soothing tones would conjure a welcoming, more casual atmosphere. Eliminating layers of molding would immediately create a lighter feeling, and moving the entrance to the dining room farther left, closer to the windows, would allow sunlight to pour in as the rooms flowed one into the other. Extending the door openings to the ceiling would highlight the scale of the rooms in a more impactful way, and a balanced mix of antique and contemporary furnishings would enliven them while still referencing the past.

Such design situations require candid discussions about what to keep and what to jettison, and I've learned that even clients who are desperate for reinvention rarely enjoy the process. It took time, but through detailed presentations I helped the couple understand that their classic prewar apartment could feel spacious, open, and light, well suited to dinner parties and entertaining family and friends. Once they were able to envision what their new home would be, they decided to donate most of their furnishings to charity and to relocate to a nearby hotel for the duration of the gut renovation.

OPPOSITE: An exuberant 18th-century gilded chair and sleek 1940s oak armchair, both French, are grouped with inlaid mother-of-pearl tables from Syria, a stone-topped game table, and a poetic Gilbert Poillerat side chair. The walls are upholstered with panels covered in a gray-blue twill, which I also used to upholster the frame of the sofa. A lightbox table that displays a trio of torsos inspired by Cambodian Angkor Wat relics glows from within.

Our transformation began in the entrance hall. I always like to make an impact in a foyer, as it sets the mood for what you are about to experience. Some designers treat this space as an afterthought, but for me it's the overture. Here, I wanted to create a crisp white box, with walls painted a bright white and floors paved in shiny white-glass tiles. Except for the library, the headers for the doors were removed and the openings brought up to the ceiling, making it seem sky-high. A fanciful vintage stool by French designer Gilbert Poillerat serves as a focal point in the room, which is anchored by a center table with an open steel base topped with frosted glass; a pair of discreet shaded sconces flank a serene abstract canvas and a 1980s upholstered Lucite bench.

In the living room, I stripped the wood parquet floors and stained them a pale driftwood color. The space needed to feel grounded, and this warm aged-wood color is always a good option. To play up the length of the room, I upholstered one wall in panels of a soft gray-blue twill and used the same fabric to cover the frame of the sofa; I like the connection between the wall and the seating. A narrow light fixture was installed just below the ceiling; it runs the length of the sofa and bathes the wall in a warm glow. The lightbox cube I designed for the corner also glows, though in a magical way that makes the carved-stone torsos placed atop it look like they are floating midair.

The furnishings are a mindful mix of old and new, as my clients wanted a modern apartment but didn't want to lose a sense of the past. I balanced elements from different periods by using clean, contemporary fabrics for the upholstery—somehow, if you cover an antique chair in a traditional fabric, it will always feel timeworn. A lyrical Poillerat side chair that I found in the Paris flea market was grouped with a stone-topped game table and a pair of Syrian inlaid mother-of-pearl tables that shimmer like delicate earrings; they mingle with an overscale gilded armchair from the 18th century and a 1940s French oak armchair.

The fireplace is a focal point in this space and my clients requested that a flat screen be installed above it. Some people are surprised to learn that I don't consider this a sacrilege, but instead I'm of the mind that if you would like a TV in your living room, you should have one. I do, however, think it's ridiculous to pretend it's not there by concealing it in some manner. Replacing the ornate mantel with a fireplace surround of white-glass panels set flush to the wall was an enormous improvement, but the most pronounced architectural alteration was to move the entrance to the dining room to the window wall. Not only did it form an enfilade with the rooms flowing into one another, allowing sunlight to flood the space, but it created a wall and corner to accommodate a capacious L-shaped sectional sofa, the most luxurious and sumptuous piece in the apartment.

I added a large clear mirror over one side of the sofa to reflect light throughout the room, while a free-form amoeba-shaped rug—woven of silk in a tone close to the driftwood-color floor—made the space feel more intimate. My clients own a lovely collection of small Impressionist drawings, including works by Gustave Courbet, Paul Gauguin, and Camille Pissarro, which I kept in their original frames. They were previously displayed throughout the apartment, but I chose to create a composition of them on

LEFT: I designed the entrance hall to make a bold, minimalist statement with snow-white walls and floors of gleaming white glass tile. The vintage table and Gilbert Poillerat stool were found in France, the framed work is by Gustave Courbet, and the Lucite bench is from the 1980s.

Design Lessons

° A foyer is far more than a place to hang coats and stash the mail. It offers an opportunity to set the mood for the house—and I think it's always important to create a surprise.

° When you are redecorating and unsure about keeping certain pieces, it's better to be brutal. Don't hem and haw—such uncertainty means you will likely eventually get rid of them. Unless something has great sentimental value, don't be hesitant to auction it, sell it, or donate it.

° Never underestimate the impact of replacing a fireplace mantel with one in a completely different style. A fireplace is often the focal point of a room and changing it can be the first serious step in the transformation of a space.

° If you want your rooms to appear taller, the best approach is to open any nonstructural doorways up to the ceiling, also removing any floor saddles between the rooms. Cleaning up or eliminating superfluous moldings can also add height to a space.

° When hanging a grouping of art, don't think in terms of a standard square—think of it as a composition that has a rhythm to it. In the living room of this apartment, I hung several Impressionist drawings in what is essentially a right angle, with the varied size of frames keeping it pleasingly off-balance. I like to lay everything out on the floor before we put a single nail in place; this helps you determine the proper scale, proportion, and distance between the artworks.

° Flat screens are easier to embrace than to hide.

ABOVE: The original living room, with its French-influenced decor. RIGHT: The ornate carved-marble mantel was replaced with panels of white glass set flush to the wall. The most impactful architectural change was streamlining the dining room entrance and moving it to the window wall, creating more generous wall space to accommodate a luxurious sectional sofa by VW Home, as well as a striking composition of my clients' collection of Impressionist drawings that were previously scattered throughout the apartment.

OPPOSITE: The center mirror, which matches one in the living room, is flanked by tall, gilded mirrors that were among the pieces my clients kept from the original decor, though I moved them here from the bedroom. The sideboard is 1940s French, the ceiling fixture is by Artemide, and I found the wonderful ostrich-egg lamp in the Paris flea market. ABOVE: I designed the chairs using a combination of fabrics—pairing a remarkable, sturdy vinyl that looks like silk with the same textile I used on the living room sofas. The painting is by Brendan Murphy.

the far wall that leads to the dining room. They have a discreet but powerful impact as a group, as they draw you in to study their beauty.

The dining room easily hosts small gatherings at a round table of my design that opens and extends to a generous oval shape that can seat 16 for dinner. The steel base is an adaptation of a stone-topped table in the living room, though this top is crafted of opaque white glass, a glossy easy-care surface that wipes clean. A large mirror is centered over the French 1940s oak sideboard; they are flanked by tall, gilded mirrors that previously hung in the primary bedroom.

The room I changed the least was the library, as I wanted it to reference the husband's past. Here, the transformation was largely achieved through color and texture. Formerly a dark, quiet room, it featured dusky paneling that we lacquered a Wedgwood blue. I think deep color in a room like this seems less intense when you use it liberally—on the walls, upholstery, and carpet. I painted the ceiling white and installed a fixture I designed to be like a strobe, bathing the space with a soft, evenly distributed light. I added a pearwood secretary, where the husband could work and keep his papers, and placed an antique Chinese cabinet under the flat screen; the Lucite chair is from the '60s.

A fresh, modern sensibility was also reflected in the bedrooms. My clients' grand-children often stay in the guest room, where I installed upholstered twin beds with a continuous headboard to make the space as easy and low-maintenance as possible. The combination is so versatile—it is perfect for children, and if you place the beds on casters, they can be easily pushed together when preferred. This layout gave my clients' guest room a more tailored, streamlined look, and we kept the window treatment simple, as well, with Roman shades that can block the morning light.

The primary bedroom is a soft, powdery cocoon. Actually, powder is exactly what I had in mind for the color palette, as I wanted the room to be the pale color of a woman's face powder—a tint so fragile it looks as if it could melt in front of your eyes. I upholstered the back wall in large rectangles of dupioni silk, with the remaining walls clad in grass cloth in the same tone. This brought texture to the space, with the wall behind the bed having a more intimate, dimensional quality to it. The bed is also upholstered, another layer of luxury, and the bed cover is a glamorous duvet that I had custom made, lighter than air and like a fluffy cloud. And though the cacophony of the city streets is just outside the windows, the bedroom is an oasis of calm, both day and night.

This was an emotional project on many levels because it was propelled by my clients wanting to create a new life together. I'll admit to feeling somewhat anxious when I opened the door to welcome them home for the first time following the renovation and installation. I was reasonably sure the wife would be pleased, as we had worked so closely together, but I wasn't convinced about the husband. The three of us had collaborated on a major transformation of a place he had called home for years. But there was no need for concern—he walked me through each room, pointing out differ-ent pieces, more excited than I could have possibly imagined. As a couple, together, they had learned to let go to move forward.

RIGHT: We preserved the library's paneling but lacquered it a Wedgwood blue, which transformed the formerly dark space. The furnishings were kept to a minimum for a tailored clean look: a wonderful pearwood secretary, antique Chinese cabinet, 1960s Lucite chair, and a pair of small tables with an ottoman; a deep sofa covered in a lush Scalamandré velvet and a silver-leafed mirror fill the niche between the bookcases.

LEFT AND ABOVE: My goal for the primary bedroom was to create an oasis of calm. The color palette, inspired by the translucent hues of face powder, is subtle and all-enveloping. The walls are papered in Larsen grass cloth, except for the wall behind the bed, which I upholstered in large rectangles of dupioni silk from Jim Thompson for added dimension. The bed and a storage ottoman at its foot are upholstered as well, and the carpet is silk. I selected two different nightstands, one made in cerused oak with an onyx top and the other crafted of bronze.

RIGHT: Upholstered twin beds by Charles H. Beckley, paired with a continuous headboard, were a good solution for the guest room, where my clients' grandchildren often stay; I used a performance fabric by Perennials for easy maintenance. We found the bedside tables at West Elm, and I was drawn to the artisanal quality of the framed African textiles, which add pattern and texture to the minimalist space.

Bright Outlook

First impressions are powerful, and the feelings I get the first time I walk through a new project often linger in my mind throughout the job until it's complete. When longtime clients purchased a Fifth Avenue penthouse in a gracious prewar building overlooking Central Park—with dramatic cityscape views to the south and lush treetop vistas across to Manhattan's West Side—I was excited to see it. But though I had arrived on a gorgeous spring day and the views were breathtaking, the place felt stodgy. Conventional. Frumpy. Old-fashioned. In short, perfect! I couldn't wait to get started.

These clients are true New Yorkers. The husband works in finance, and the wife is a writer and musician who is involved in a range of cultural activities. I designed their previous apartment about 15 years prior; it was a rather dark, rambling duplex on Park Avenue that functioned like a country house. Decorated in a traditional style, it had served as a comfortable home for their kids, nannies, and various pets, but now that their children were adults, my clients were eager for an adventure. Having compromised on views and light to get the proper square footage in which to raise their family, they craved dazzling views, nonstop sunlight and brilliant sunsets, and a glamorous space that reflected both the energy of the city and the vitality of this next stage of their lives.

My design brief was to transform the 1920s three-bedroom apartment into a minimalist, free-flowing space—an elegant setting to entertain family and friends, with bright-white walls to accommodate my clients' burgeoning art collection. The wife wanted it to feel fresh and modern but to include elements from the past, mixing new pieces with existing furnishings. These pieces, refinished and reupholstered, became the jewels of the interiors. We also decided to flip the floor plan, moving the kitchen from the east side of the apartment to the west, for its park views, and she requested a dressing room for the relocated primary suite and a library in place of the extra bedrooms.

I approached the project like a surgeon, reappropriating space as needed, moving walls, and eliminating odd juts and nooks and crannies. Low arches, moldings, beams, and window casements were banished, most door openings were extended to the ceiling, and walls were aligned. While preserving the integrity of the original architecture, these alterations enabled me to create clear, continuous sightlines and rooms that flow seamlessly from one to the next.

To maximize the light and reflect the sparkle of the city, walls and ceilings were spray-painted a high-gloss white, except for the library, which was coated in an iridescent teal. My clients are drawn to art with intense color, and both the deep blue-green tones of the library and the bright hues of their art collection cut through the surrounding sea

OPPOSITE: A curvaceous Vladimir Kagan mohair sofa and a cocktail table that I custom designed soften a corner of the living room; the carved-sandstone torsos are from VW Home. In place of formal window treatments, I installed Roman shades throughout the apartment; those shown here are fashioned of a sheer linen gauze.

of white with the sharpness of a horizon, a powerful and compelling contrast.

Gleaming white glass–tile floors pave the foyer and hall leading to the library and bedroom suite, as well as the kitchen and breakfast area, unifying the public and private spaces of the apartment. I emphasized the square dimensions of the foyer by dropping the ceiling to install a square inset grid of LED strip lighting; it lends an ethereal feeling to a space punctuated by striking art and a vintage bench.

The sun-splashed living room offers views to the south, east, and west, and opens to a terrace overlooking the park. We placed a beautiful antique Tabriz carpet from my clients' previous apartment on an angle, as well as all the furniture and the piano, a move that fools the eye to make the space seem even bigger. I designed a glass-top cocktail table as a reference to Central Park—its steel base is meant to resemble crisscrossed tree branches as they lean against each other—and a streamlined chaise longue that extends from the corner. Several pieces from the Park Avenue home were recovered for a less fussy, more contemporary look, and midcentury classics now mingle with the vintage and antique accessories.

Though I originally planned to enlarge the opening to the library to pour light into the hallway, a riser on one side would have made it off-balance. Instead, we created a faux second riser to flank the doorway and added shelving that is open to both the room and the hall. To add dimension and detail to the space—and inspired by a 1920s photo I discovered in a vintage design book—I added very narrow shelves around the perimeter of the room, lighting just the top row. This space now sparkles like a gem, and with a deep blue Pierre Paulin Ribbon chair sitting sculpturelike in front of the terrace doors, it's a bold counterpoint to the pristine white apartment.

Not only was the primary suite's original bathroom an interior space that lacked any natural light, but it was also modest in size, and any expansion would be complicated by the co-op's stringent construction rules limiting the addition of a "wet" area with plumbing where one didn't previously exist. I realized we could relocate the adjacent laundry room to accommodate the bathtub and enlarged shower and repurpose a former closet for a built-in dressing table. To create a sense of visual openness and allow natural light to spill in from the surrounding rooms, I had the door and exterior walls crafted using panels of frosted glass.

I'm not known for using pattern in my interiors, but there's a poetic, mercurial quality to Fortuny prints from Italy that I love, and I upholstered one wall each of both the bedroom and dressing/sitting room in a beautiful silver-platinum pattern. In the bedroom, the silvery tones repeat the shimmer of a vintage antiqued-mirror desk found at an estate sale, with an overall effect that is serene, soothing, and sybaritic.

Though I have never considered decamping from either my Manhattan loft or my beach house in Montauk, both of which I deeply love, I must admit that this penthouse gave me pause—the views are extraordinary, and you feel like you're on top of the world. I believe my clients share my feelings, perhaps proof that what once felt old-fashioned and stodgy is now truly sensational.

LEFT: The foyer's walls and ceiling were spray-painted in PPG's Delicate White in satin and high-gloss finishes, respectively, and the space is illuminated by an inset grid of LED lights. Though I removed moldings throughout the apartment, the carved millwork framing the door to the paneled dining room, at right, was wonderful and I liked the contrast it brought to the minimalist space. The collage, left, is by Zhuang Hong-yi, the painting on the far wall is by Jens Fänge, and the neon work at right is by Beverly Fishman; the vintage bench is from VW Home.

LEFT: I designed the upholstered chaise longue with a mirror-finished I-beam–style base; it is flanked by a 17th-century Flemish chair and a vintage George Nelson for Herman Miller tray table—both found on 1stDibs— and a Platner armchair by Knoll.

RIGHT: We installed a narrow grid of track lights, as the room's concrete ceiling precluded recessed lighting, and though I set the furnishings and rug on an angle, I like that the grid creates a linear framework within the space. I mixed new pieces with my custom designs and elements from my clients' previous apartment—a VW Home wing chair, a French Rococo chair newly upholstered in a Kyle Bunting hair on hide, a Bridgewater chair by Jonas reupholstered in a luxe Loro Piana wool, as well as a beautiful antique Tabriz rug from Doris Leslie Blau.

ABOVE: To maximize the contrast of the color-saturated library with the crisp whiteness of the surrounding rooms, the entrance is flanked by shelves that are open to both the library and the adjacent hallway, which displays a vibrant abstract work by Bernard Frize. The bronze torso is by Anita Huffington. RIGHT: I felt the library and media room should be warm and intimate, with more detail than the cool minimalism elsewhere in the apartment. Inspired by the narrow decorative shelves in a 1920s-era room I once saw in a vintage design book, I applied trim linear rows of wood around the perimeter of the space; they add interest without looking fussy, and the top row is lit to throw light to the ceiling in a subtle, glamorous way. The room's color palette was designed to reflect the brilliant blue sky and lush Central Park trees visible from its windows and terrace, with walls painted an iridescent teal blue and furnishings and a carpet in complementary tones of blue and green. A pull-out sofa, upholstered in a peacock-blue silk mohair, was added to accommodate guests, and a stone-topped, ebonized wooden cube and a custom leather-upholstered ottoman with recessed casters serve as cocktail tables. The desk is built-in, with a wooden top and mirror-finished C-clamp–shaped metal supports; the leather Thom chairs are from VW Home. Pierre Paulin's Ribbon chair, from M2L, is a 1960s design that will forever seem timeless to me.

LEFT: A former dressing room was repurposed as a breakfast room adjacent to the kitchen. My client suggested that we employ a neoclassical bench from her previous apartment, which I paired with a pedestal table and Panton chairs from Design Within Reach; the suspension light is by Artemide. The work displayed near the window is by Evan Lorberbaum, and the pencil drawing leaning against the wall is by Marisa Green.
ABOVE: We painted the dining room's boiserie, which was in worn condition, and refinished the floor with a neutral earthy taupe stain. The arched bookshelves were squared off, and the shelves backed in a silver-foil paper by Maya Romanoff to softly reflect sunlight during the day and candlelight in the evening. This is an idea I saw many years ago in a house in New Orleans, one that has stayed in my mind ever since. The ceiling fixture is by David Weeks, and we updated the table and chairs from my clients' previous dining room with the table in a darker tone and the seating reupholstered—the armchairs in leather and the side chairs in a sturdy mohair. The bronze sculpture is by Antoine Poncet, and the aquatint etching is by Robert Motherwell.

Terrace

Terrace

Bath

Dressing Room

Bedroom

Family Room

F.P.

Living Room

Primary Bedroom

F.P.

CL

CL

WIC

CL

Hallway

CL

CL

WIC

CL

WIC

Hallway

CL

Bath

Laundry

W/D

Entry

Entry

Terrace

Dining Room

REF

Kitchen

D/W

CL

Pantry

Bath

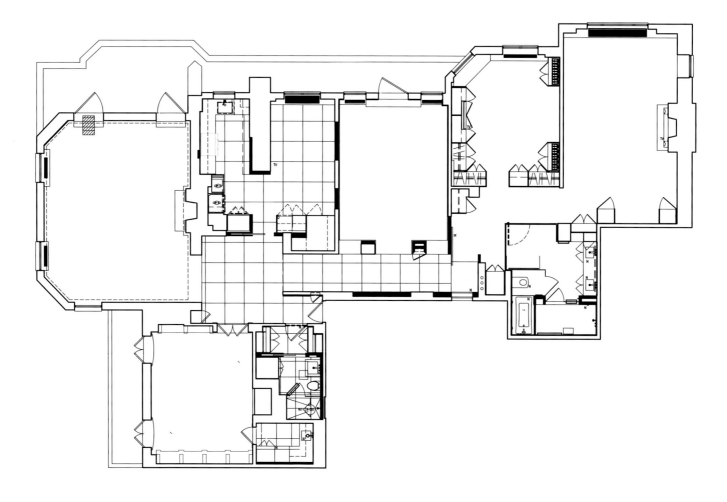

Design Lessons

◦ When you start a project, make a list of the positive and negative aspects of the space—sometimes, just correcting the negatives can produce the most satisfying result.

◦ Adding a floating shelf to a narrow foyer creates an unobtrusive spot to leave your keys and place a small vase of flowers or a scented candle. Also, since it doesn't take up floor space this can make an entrance hall feel larger.

◦ Transform a long hallway into a vista, with a sightline that ends at a striking artwork displayed on the far wall.

◦ A dining table needn't aways be parallel with windows or walls. It's unexpected to place it on an angle, and depending on the shape of the room, doing so might allow the space to accommodate a larger table.

◦ I like to incorporate the bathtub inside the shower space, instead of subdividing the room. Putting them together makes the entire space seem bigger.

◦ If you have an interior bathroom with no natural light, consider using frosted-glass walls to allow sunlight from adjacent rooms to spill in. Light flowing through frosted glass always gives the sense of a window, even when one doesn't exist.

LEFT: I created a dreamy, sybaritic space for my clients' bedroom and dressing room/sitting area, using the wife's favorite lavender hue. A classic tufted daybed is the centerpiece of the space, which I mixed with a mohair-upholstered Metropolitan chair by B&B Italia; an 18th-century French painted table, which served as a nightstand in their former home; an octagonal inlaid side table from VW Home; and a Saarinen side table by Knoll. The upholstered walls here and in the bedroom are clad in a subtle geometric print by Fortuny.

OPPOSITE: I like to be able to see a bed as soon as I walk into a bedroom, but here the fireplace wall faced the door, and I had no choice but to place the bed facing the mantel. My solution was to install a massive 4-foot-wide by 8-foot-tall carved and gilded mirror that reflects the bed straight-on, instead of in profile. **ABOVE:** We wanted the bathroom, an interior space, to feel spacious and light, which was enormously challenging. We devised a creative solution by relocating the adjacent laundry in order to install the bathtub within an open shower area, and we commandeered space from an extra closet to create a glamorous built-in makeup area. Light now flows in from the hall and surrounding rooms via a frosted glass–paneled door and walls; we also used frosted glass for an interior window to the shower area. The frosted glass magically conjures the feeling of windows where none exist.

Design Challenges

Maybe it's my strong survival instinct, but I love a good challenge. When given limitations of budget or space, I believe you can rise to your best possible level—though I'll admit I'm not as keen on situations that involve a fast turnaround and not enough time.

I'm perhaps most proud of projects that ended up being seriously difficult for a variety of reasons, and the lessons I learned by overcoming those obstacles have been put to use countless times since. Plus, money has nothing to do with good design—a big budget might offer more options, but never underestimate the beauty of found objects, flea-market treasures, and a white canvas slipcover.

The Dreaming Room

It is ironic that though creating a room for a designer show house might entail an insanely tight schedule and endless list of constraints, this type of project is among my most liberating because there's no client. In addition, show houses raise funds for worthy causes, while engaging a design-focused crowd of potential clients; I also love the blue-sky thinking and fiscal ingenuity they require. Some designers spend a fortune, but my sense is the cheaper you can do it, the better—the purpose is to offer ideas and show how inventive you are.

The Kips Bay Decorator Show House is long considered the most prestigious in America, and I've participated in a few iterations over the years, including a space for the 1991 house that rocket-fueled my solo career when it made the cover of *Metropolitan Home*. I happily accepted an invitation to create a room for the 2019 Manhattan show house, and when the floor plans and scouting photos arrived, I selected the breakfast room; it was a manageable size and opened to a garden off the kitchen.

When I actually saw the room in person, it was truly awful—dark, dingy, and depressing! It would be a huge challenge to create something memorable and impactful without investing thousands of dollars, and with just weeks till opening day, I needed a plan.

The room was clad in painted paneling, with a marble fireplace, a pair of windows, and a door that led outside. I knew for sure that I wanted to use the color aubergine, which was hugely popular in the 1980s. Now rather uncommon, the hue would not only stand out, but it would also surprise anyone who might associate me with minimalist white interiors. And since we had to provide access to the garden, I designed a curved path of faux grass to bisect the room, not yet knowing what else I would do. Then Kohler offered to donate a sculptural bathtub, prompting my decision to conjure the "Dreaming Room"—a fantasy retreat to take a long bath, read a book, look at beautiful things, and dream.

The project took shape. We painted the floors glossy black; the Shade Store fashioned curtain panels of a romantic, gossamer gauze; and I had a glamorous pouf upholstered in silk velvet. The centerpiece of the space was a Kohler freestanding soaking bathtub positioned atop a dramatic Cambria-quartz platform. Two floor-to-ceiling mirrors and an array of furniture and accessories from VW Home made the setting feel layered and complete.

With its deep, saturated color, this was a an especially calming room, and it offered a sense of tranquility that I found very interesting. And though, to me, the concept behind a show house room is to make a bold, inspiring statement without the restrictions posed by pragmatism and functionality, I could easily imagine designing a Dreaming Room for a client. There's a distinct pleasure to be found in creating a wonderful fantasy space, but it's even more gratifying when that fantasy can become a reality.

OPPOSITE: For the 2019 Kips Bay Decorator Show House in New York, I designed a space I called the "Dreaming Room," which featured aubergine walls and Kohler bath fixtures.

Design Lessons

○ You can use old pieces in a room without having them look old. For example, except for the bath fixtures and platform, nearly every other piece in this space has a sense of history to it yet still looks fresh because of the mix.

○ Painting a room a dark hue won't make it a dark room. High-gloss paint and reflective surfaces help to create the impression of lightness, and using white as a contrast gives the eye a bright focal point.

○ Unexpected, inventive lighting solutions can add a sense of drama. To accentuate the wall color in the Kips Bay room, I installed a thin strip of LED lights around the perimeter of the space. Attached to the baseboards just above the floor, it created almost an ombré effect, with the light bathing the walls from the ground up.

○ If you want to display a small-scale artwork over a fireplace, don't center it—hanging it off-center will have a stronger effect and look more interesting.

○ Never underestimate the importance of using greenery in a room; trees, plants, and flowers add energy and warmth.

○ When possible, consider floating your bathtub within the room—it adds instant glamour to a space.

LEFT: Sheer curtain panels made by the Shade Store serve as an ethereal foil to the color-saturated walls. The 18th-century Bodhisattva statue, Chinese console, and marble tray are from VW Home; John Salibello loaned the vintage Karl Springer vanity mirror, and the Gaston Lachaise sculpture is from my personal collection. I used a small army of lady's slipper orchids in moss-covered clay pots to make a stronger impact. Kohler's donation of their Ceric cast-resin freestanding bathtub and Loure polished-chrome floor-mounted tub filler spearheaded my decision to create this luxurious bathroom.

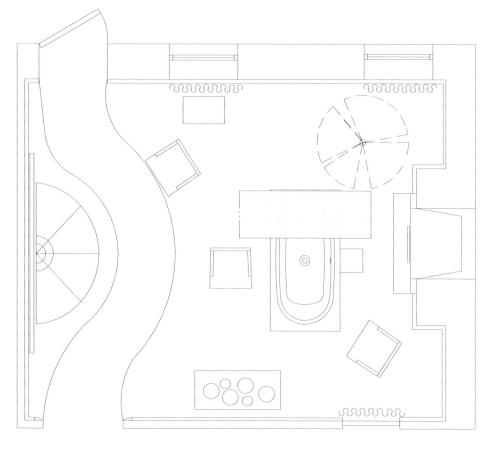

ABOVE, FROM TOP: A "before" photo of what was formerly the townhouse's breakfast room; the mantel was the sole redeeming element in the space. The Dreaming Room floor plan. RIGHT: The Kohler tub was mounted atop a raised platform crafted of Huntley engineered quartz by Cambria, a counterpoint to the gleaming, black-painted floor. The silvered Indian wedding chair and the French 1940s armchairs—upholstered in Fortuny's Simboli fabric—are from VW Home. The photo displayed over the mantel is by Hellen van Meene, and I used a rippling panel of mirrored Lucite from Canal Plastics to add an unexpected dimension to the space.

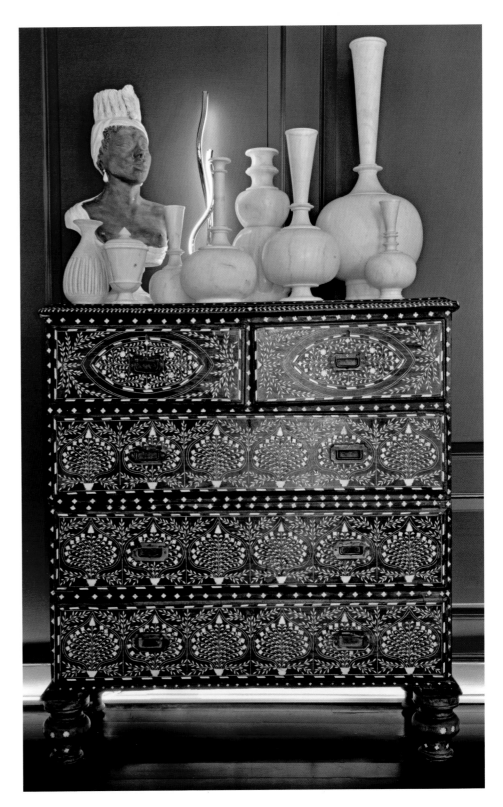

LEFT: Because my room provided access to a terrace off the adjacent kitchen, I created a curved path of faux turf to connect my room and the garden. The semicircular pouf was upholstered in a deep-eggplant velvet and the side table and floor lamp are by Cedric Hartman; a Paul Outerbridge photo is displayed against a monumental custom mirror by APF Munn. The entire bottom perimeter of the room was illuminated to bathe the space with a warm wash of light, a subtle but highly effective solution. ABOVE: I grouped a 1940s clay-and-porcelain bust found in a French flea market with a collection of hand-carved marble vessels I designed; the accessories and inlaid chest are from VW Home.

Friendly Persuasion

People often warn that you should never work with friends. I, however, have developed longtime friendships with several clients and, not long ago, I had a wonderful experience helping a good friend, Shelley Washington, with her Austin, Texas, home. When you work with a friend, you do it for love, and we overcame the dual challenges of a relatively modest budget and distance—we live across the country from one another. In fact, the first time I actually saw the house in person was at the installation.

Shelley and I met through my friend Twyla Tharp when Shelley was a lead dancer in her dance company, and I've designed a few of Shelley's homes over the years. Now a dance master who stages Twyla Tharp Dance performances around the world, Shelley and her husband, David Swenson, a noted Ashtanga yoga master, split their time between a cottage-style home in Texas and a place in Hawaii.

After living in the Austin house for a few years, they found its layout was too compartmentalized and not functioning well to meet their needs. Shelley first came to me for help with a kitchen redesign, but when I saw the floor plan, I told her, "The problem is, you're going to have a great kitchen in a not-so-great house." Shelley and David eventually agreed, and the project developed into a complete reconfiguration of the first floor and renovations throughout—including a new kitchen, stripping out humdrum millwork and moldings, refinishing the floors, and updating the bathrooms.

This was pre-pandemic but even then, working strictly long-distance proved less problematic than one might think. Shelley sent me photos of the entire house, but I often prefer to design from just a floor plan because it only shows the outline of the space. Instead of getting stuck on what currently exists, I am able to envision what is possible. And I discovered a time-saving benefit of working from a distance—you deal only with what's necessary on a call and then you can hang up!

Shelley hired a measuring service to provide necessary specifications and found a good local contractor. We sent samples back and forth and had regular FaceTime walk-throughs, but the outcome was so successful primarily because Shelley and David are exacting, precise people and they were brilliant at managing the project.

Though from the exterior the house still looks like a charming cottage, inside it feels fresh and modern. We created a serene, calm space for relaxing and entertaining, a home that is now a true refuge for its globe-trotting owners. Shelley regularly tells me, "I feel so lucky; I love it, I love it, I love it." And for me, the house is a good example of a budget spent wisely—it reflects great style, but without a big price tag. Even better, Shelley and I are still best friends.

OPPOSITE: We purposefully kept the living room's monumental painted-wood fireplace to lend a sense of continuity with the original interior. I like that it has a soft, somewhat crusty quality to it; it looks timeworn, which provides a wonderful contrast when paired with a crisp, pristine background.

LEFT: We opened the wall separating the staircase from the sitting room, creating an ethereal, intimate space with double-height ceilings. This is the only room with drapery, and the translucent floor-to-ceiling curtains accentuate the soaring ceiling to great effect. The slipcovered club chairs and overscale gilded mirror are from RH/Restoration Hardware, as is much of the furniture in the house; the pieces work well here, and it was convenient for us to shop their website and confer on selections long-distance.

RIGHT: The house was charming, but its first-floor layout was poorly allocated, and the living area, which was situated on the far side of the staircase and opened onto the kitchen, lacked any sense of definition. Because the staircase wall was surprisingly short, extending it enabled us to create an inviting living room by expanding the seating area. In addition, we installed picture ledges as a solution to display Shelley and David's photography collection. They were hesitant to use picture hooks once we had painted the walls a semigloss white and the ledges offer the flexibility to move pieces around.

LEFT: The living room seating area is illuminated by recessed lighting fixtures that were installed within the structural beams of the existing ceiling; we also cut a square opening at the far end of the wall, which allows light to pass through from the sitting room. Sliding glass doors lead to a spacious deck and offer leafy views that provide a warm contrast to the cool palette within; when unfurled, the Roman shades are semitransparent, providing both privacy and light. Art and artifacts found on the couple's travels, including a carved-wood Buddha from Thailand, are displayed throughout their home.

RIGHT: A nonessential portion of the wall between the kitchen and dining area was removed to make the space more open and cohesive. I've never much liked floating a dining table and chairs in the center of a room, and pairing them with a curved banquette in the corner of the dining area makes the layout seem more spacious. Plus, the banquette is comfortable for two, or you can seat as many as eight all together. We used a restaurant-supply table base and asked the kitchen cabinetmaker to craft a top; the banquette is upholstered in an easy-care gunmetal vinyl that has the look of silk.

LEFT AND ABOVE: Shelley loves to cook and wanted a kitchen that felt airy yet connected to the adjacent living and dining areas. I reoriented the layout 90 degrees. A local cabinetmaker built out the space, which I wanted to keep bright and white, with nearly seamless flush cabinet doors to blend in more easily. White Glassos counters and backsplashes and pale wood floors keep the palette cool; the refrigerator is by Sub-Zero, and the Bottega counter stools are from Design Within Reach.

BEFORE

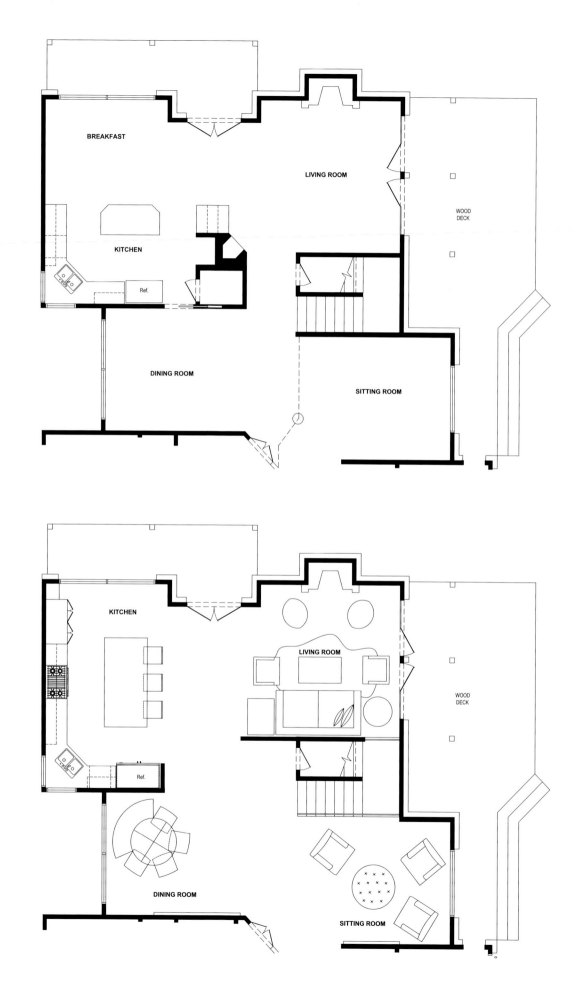

AFTER

Design Lessons

- When selecting furnishings for a room, study the elements that are in the space already and use those colors as the foundation of your palette.

- I always install curtains and shades at ceiling height, even if there is wall space over the window. It provides a cleaner line and creates the illusion that the window is larger than it is.

- A wall niche is the perfect place to create a pleasing vignette, one that gives your eye a place to rest.

- Floating a bath cabinet will make the room feel bigger; mirroring the entire wall behind the cabinet will amplify the space even more.

- Keeping window treatments relatively simple and spare instantly invites more light into a room; it allows a space to glow.

- A banquette—either built-in or freestanding—provides comfortable seating and frees up floor space as it minimizes the distance between a table and the wall. Keep in mind that the table should overhang the banquette by three inches.

RIGHT: The primary bedroom is a serene, sun-splashed space. Pre-renovation, there was a maze of HVAC ductwork overhead, but we were able to open and square-off the ceiling where it was duct-free to create the illusion of height. My plan to upholster the wall behind the bed was scuttled by Shelley's cat, who likes to climb; instead, we opted to paint it a soft blue. The piped bed linens are by Matouk, and the bed is a design I created for RH/Restoration Hardware.

OPPOSITE: Shelley craved a spacious, luxurious bathroom and had long been disappointed in the small size of the original primary bath. We were able to annex the adjacent closet and installed a sliding door to maximize space. And even though the existing arched window was overscale, I added a skylight to bring in even more natural light. The twin sinks are installed in a wall-to-wall vanity that I floated above the floor, which is clad in 36-inch-square white Glassos tiles, as are the walls. **ABOVE:** The room is a veritable sea of white, including a 1940s flea-market slipper chair that sports a flirtatious terrycloth slipcover laced across the back like a ballet costume.

RIGHT: Additional bedrooms now serve as offices for both Shelley and David, as well as a yoga studio; Shelley's space, in particular, is one of my favorites. It has leafy treetop views and looks a bit spare, furnished with disparate furniture and objects that have traveled with her from house to house. We fashioned her desk from an old tabletop that we attached to a pair of white pedestals and the armchairs are vintage Walters Wicker designs. It's a space that to me looks like nothing there was meant to belong, but somehow everything came together.

Sunshine State

When clients purchase a vacation home after falling head-over-heels in love with its breathtaking views, how to furnish it is often the last thing on their minds. One of the challenges for me is that by the time I see their property, what was at first an afterthought has become the priority.

Recently, longtime clients purchased a dramatic three-bedroom oceanfront condo with a wraparound terrace in a striking Miami building designed by famed Italian architect Renzo Piano. Perched high above the cerulean sea, the apartment's views are spectacular, a fact the real estate developers hoped to maximize with an open floor plan in the main living area. In reality, the loftlike design created a situation that I considered less than ideal. The front door opens to the living area of the apartment, a large room with a kitchen at one end, the terrace at the other, and the primary suite and guest rooms at either end—a volume of space that needed to accommodate cooking, dining, seating, and entertaining. With the endless expanse of water seen through the windows and little sense of architectural separation within, I was concerned that the large room needed a sense of structure and purpose—though without building walls that would obscure the glorious ocean views.

My solution was to devise a floor-to-ceiling angled screen constructed of narrow wooden slats and stainless-steel tubing that now delineates the rectangular seating area from the kitchen and dining area. The idea came to me on a beach walk in Montauk, when I noticed a house with a deck shaded by a slatted roof—I realized a screen could provide a sense of separation and privacy yet still allow the ocean to be in full view. The screen's impact is to create what feels like two sun-splashed spaces that fulfill multiple purposes, a perfect balance between separation and openness.

An empty living room offers a blank canvas and the freedom to play with unexpected shapes and surfaces. In this case, I designed a slightly angled sofa so everyone seated could enjoy the view, and mixed curvaceous 1960s and '70s chairs with tables and white leather ottomans of my design. An extraordinary sculptural work by Ghanaian artist Serge Attukwei Clottey, crafted of melted and stitched fragments of yellow plastic gallon jugs, is displayed on one wall; the shot of electric color makes the room shine.

Since the building was new construction, we felt no need to move walls or alter the baths and kitchen. I designed the bedroom suites to be quiet and serene, and we painted the primary bedroom and guest rooms in hues of soft white and pale blue; wherever possible mirrors reflect the water and sky. Though my design brief was to create a carefree retreat for my clients, my focus—like theirs—was always on the view.

OPPOSITE: I love the energy created by the juxtaposition of color and texture in this Miami living room, featuring a woven-rattan chair, seagrass carpet, and a remarkable assemblage by Ghanaian artist Serge Attukwei Clottey, which adds rich color to the otherwise monochromatic space.

PRECEDING PAGES: A floor-to-ceiling wood-slatted screen separates the living room from the kitchen and dining area in what was formerly a wide-open space; the sofa was angled to make the most of the ocean view to the left. An egglike Esfera chair from Espasso and a pair of Palla chairs by Bonacina, bold designs from the 1960s and '70s, mix with leather-covered cubes and stone-topped tables of my design. **LEFT:** In the dining area, an upholstered banquette is grouped with a butter-yellow resin-top table and my Web Collection dining chairs from VW Home.

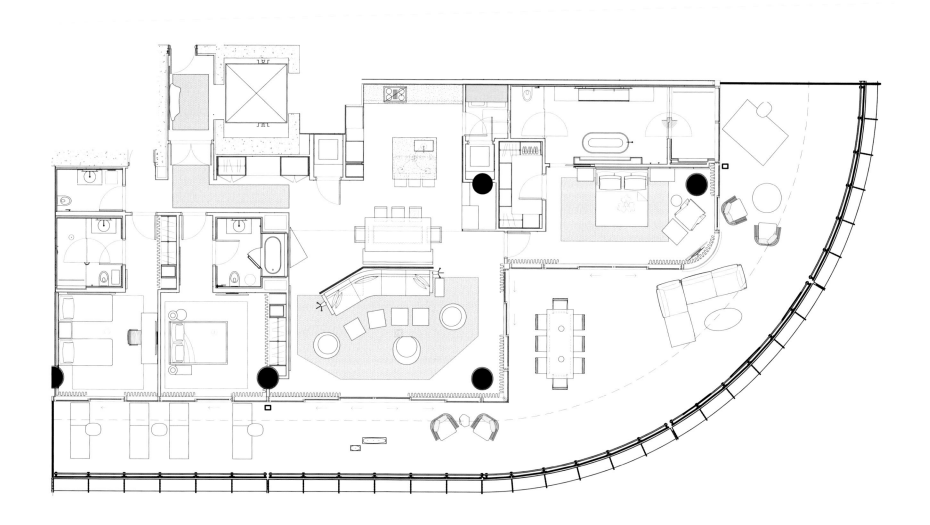

Design Lessons

- I'm a big believer in carefree living at the beach—including sturdy performance fabrics that withstand water, sand, and soil, and surfaces requiring little upkeep. Interiors should be relaxing, not stressful, and I try to avoid anything fragile or precious.

- Sometimes I remove nonessential walls to open up a space, and in other situations I create a separation or the idea of a wall without blocking the light or a view. In this condo apartment, I used a screen of narrow wood slats; a curtain—either sheer or solid—can provide a similar effect.

- When planning the lighting for a room with windows that face an expanse of water, keep in mind that the view essentially will turn pitch-black once the sun goes down, unlike city views that sparkle in the evening, or a suburban or country home vista that might have ambient light from neighboring houses. Sheer curtains will help to mitigate the darkness and multiple sources of soft interior lighting will compensate for the murky view; if there is a terrace, it can be subtly lit to bounce light within.

- I like guest rooms that have a sense of individuality and I use different elements and colors to set them apart.

- I often use a panel of polished stainless steel as an alternative to mirrored glass, as I did in the primary bedroom of this apartment. I love the romantic reflection it casts; it's soft but still precise.

RIGHT: One of the guest rooms features a continuous headboard, which I find to be extremely practical; the beds are on casters and can be placed together if preferred when a couple visits. A trio of rustic Indonesian window transoms are displayed above the beds, and we installed three mirrors horizontally on the wall facing the window to reflect the ocean vista and visually expand the rather compact space.

LEFT AND ABOVE: The windows in the primary suite's bedroom wrap the distinctive curve of the building. The focus here is on luxurious comfort, the ocean views, and the reflection of the water and sky throughout the space. The wall behind the bed is clad in cerused oak inset with panels of polished stainless steel to lend a soft mirrored effect; floating nightstands flank the upholstered headboard, which features reading lights that discreetly flip up for use, like those on an airplane seat.

From Basic to Bespoke

A few years ago, a young Chicago couple commissioned me to help them furnish their under-construction townhouse in the city's Lincoln Park neighborhood; the wife was an executive at an advertising firm and her husband, also in advertising, was an art director and copywriter. When a local magazine published the project not long after it was completed and the husband was asked to write the story, he generously described my work as "elegant yet informal, modern yet timeless, minimal yet warm"—a characterization that I couldn't help but love.

The townhouse project, however, had posed a few major challenges from the outset, including a rather modest budget and the lean, compact footprint of the structure itself. The property's original 100-year-old house, which was in disrepair, had been taken down. To keep construction costs in line my clients decided to build in its place a straightforward transitional-style home with a basic layout and conventional architectural details; my purview would be furnishing the first floor and an upstairs media room.

For a long-distance project, it was definitely small-scale but I accepted the assignment because I had made a connection with the husband a decade earlier, when he visited my showroom, VW Home, on a business trip to New York City. After telling me how much he admired my design aesthetic and that he hoped someday to hire me, he stayed in touch, buying a few pieces from the showroom from time to time, and eventually he and his wife contacted me when construction on their new house was underway. Liking a good challenge, I said yes.

The house was already about 75 percent built when the couple asked me to review the plans, but I wasn't deterred from voicing strong opinions and I'm pretty sure my first site visit left their heads spinning. They were such a cool, creative couple, with young kids, and I sensed they were compromising on the overall design scheme—crown moldings and coffered ceilings made a statement that was ordinary, not innovative.

That game-changing first site visit also resulted in the primary bedroom, study, powder room, and overall lighting plan being added to my design brief; the couple would still mastermind their children's rooms. A few months later, I presented my floor plans and proposed furnishings to them—an experience the husband described in the magazine article as, "Our brains promptly exploded. Everything we expected was there, but none of it in the way we expected." That must have been a good thing, as they literally posted much of their old furniture for sale online shortly after.

Even though my suggested changes for the first floor weren't drastic, the effects were dramatic. We nixed the prosaic moldings, removed the door headers, and took down

OPPOSITE: A vignette in the dining area of a townhouse in Chicago's Lincoln Park neighborhood features a 16th-century glazed-earthenware vessel from Thailand and a trio of sculptural topiaries.

the wall separating the parlor from the dining room, which created a loftlike space that would be divided by a floor-to-ceiling open bookcase. Parlor-floor rooms in narrow townhouses often seem more like passageways, and transforming two small, contiguous rooms into one made the overall area look and feel much larger. The front door now leads to a sitting area, which is used primarily when they have cocktail parties, and the dining area—the larger of the two spaces—is on the opposite side of the bookshelves.

When dealing with limited square footage, creative solutions can fool the eye and make a big difference. For instance, I designed the bookshelves here to be wide enough to define a line of demarcation but not limit the flow of the room, and in the dining area I paired a corner banquette with a round dining table and open-frame armchairs to maximize every free inch. A freestanding table surrounded by chairs would have required significantly more space, and I wanted to keep an open passageway from the front rooms back to the kitchen and den, amplifying the entire area. And, sadly, one idea never made it to fruition: To make these spaces seem wider, I specified that the floor planks should be laid to run across the width of the house instead of its length. The contractor adamantly refused because "lengthwise is the way it's always done," and after a heated argument I begrudgingly lost the battle.

The kitchen and den serve as the hub of the house, command central for the busy life of a young family. I designed the kitchen cabinetry in oak, and in place of standard panel cabinets, I inset a narrow band of stainless steel as a distinctive border. The marble-topped center island was crafted of mahogany for contrast and boasts a traditional silhouette; we built a stainless-steel box underneath to camouflage sink plumbing, the dishwasher, and storage.

A window niche was employed as a breakfast area, with wood shutters and a gauzy linen shade providing privacy from the neighboring house while allowing sunlight to filter into the room. Just beyond, the kitchen is open to the den, where we designed the built-in cabinetry flanking the fireplace to be the same height as the kitchen counters and island for a continuous sight line.

Upstairs, the generously sized primary bedroom is a moody, seductive space. We used a soothing gunmetal tone throughout, as my clients requested a dark color palette, though I added an overscale silver-leafed mirror to reflect light from the windows and prevent a cavernlike feeling.

I clad one wall of the top-floor media room in an interesting cork wall covering with glints of metallic silver; I like a mix of textures to add interest in a monochromatic space. The deep sofa stretches wall-to-wall, and the armchairs swivel to face the television, which was specially mounted to float in front of the curtained stair hall.

Less than a year after our first site visit, I installed all the furnishings and invited my clients home for the reveal—beautiful flowers, flickering candlelight, and soft jazz are always part of my ritual. The verdict from the writer husband who had waited a decade for this moment? He and his wife were as thrilled as I'd hoped they would be—proof that even a challenging project can turn out to be the home of someone's dreams.

LEFT: The parlor-floor living and dining rooms were reconfigured as part of my design plan for the narrow space, creating this sitting room/gallery area just inside the front door. Armchairs from VW Home are grouped around a custom-made round pouf, which centers the room and makes the space seem airier; the cowhide rugs are from Edelman. Picture rails installed on the far wall display paintings, sculpture, and works on paper from my clients' collection.

ABOVE AND RIGHT: A floor-to-ceiling open bookcase serves as a dividing line between the two spaces while allowing sunlight to spill across the entire room. In the dining area, I paired an inlaid Indian chair with an antique painted table from China; the photographs are by Malia Jensen. A Brno armchair by Mies van der Rohe for Knoll and a VW Home dining table are nestled with a corner banquette to amplify the open floor space.

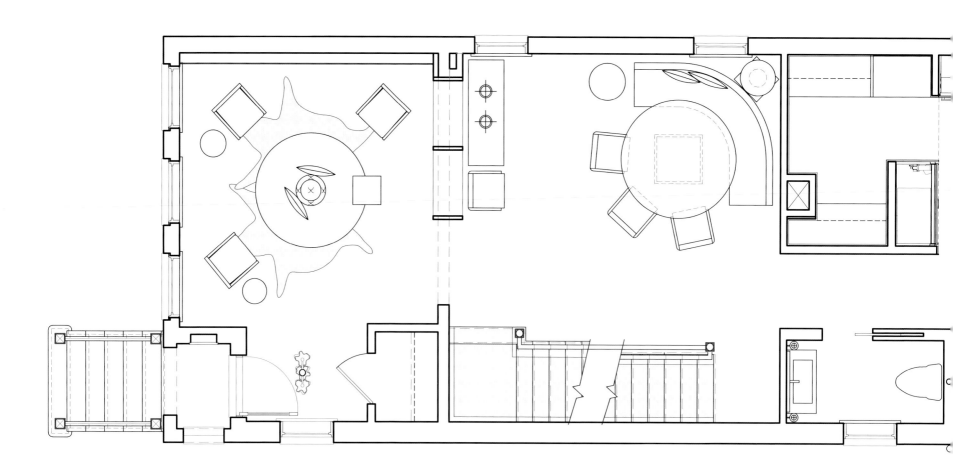

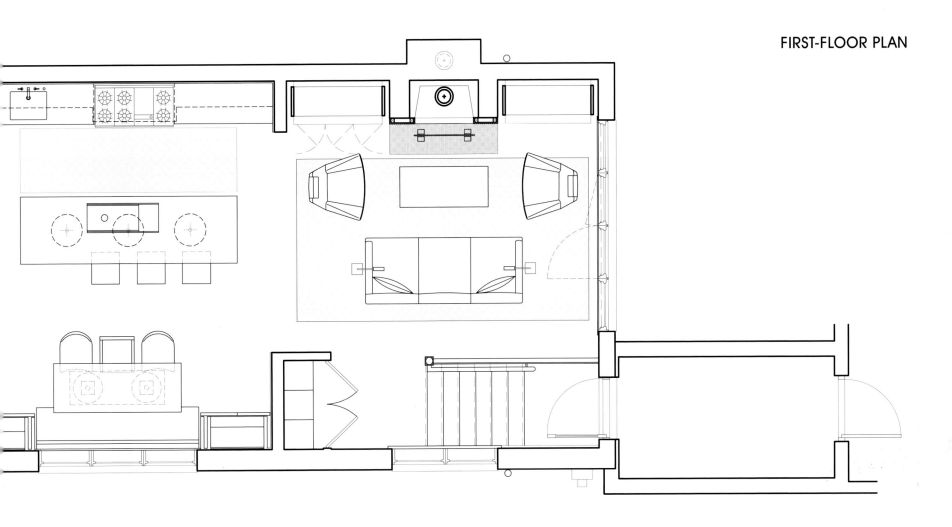

Design Lessons

- When faced with the challenge of an odd layout, narrow rooms, or limited square footage, settling for the status quo is not an option; don't be afraid to go for the unexpected. Completely reinterpreting the existing floor plan might offer some surprising solutions.

- Small spaces benefit from a consistent, monochromatic palette. Complementary color should flow from the front door all the way through; the more you break it up, the smaller the space will feel.

- Schoolhouse window shades—shades that can be opened from the top or the bottom—are a brilliant solution when sunlight and privacy are in equal demand. I used them in the sitting room of this townhouse and realized how beautiful it is to see leafy tree branches outside the window.

- Built-in banquettes are the saviors of small dining rooms and breakfast areas.

- I like to create a cocoon of color and often design a room's walls and floors or carpet to be the same color. It doesn't always have to be just one hue—you can mix tones—but I prefer serenity to a cacophony.

LEFT: The back of the townhouse comprises an open-plan kitchen, a breakfast area, and a den that function well within a relatively compact space. The large marble-topped island combines a polished-mahogany framework with a core clad in stainless steel, which reflects light and brightens the surrounding area. The custom-made cabinets are inset with a sleek ribbon of stainless steel, the counters and backsplash were crafted of white glass tile, and the professional-style range is by Wolf; the Lem Piston counter stools are from Design Within Reach. ABOVE: We created a breakfast area within the window niche, which is flanked by additional storage cabinets; wood shutters and a linen Roman shade filter sunlight and provide privacy from the neighboring house.

RIGHT: The kitchen is adjacent to the den, which features bookcases that I backlit for a touch of drama. The minimalist hearth is sheathed in slate. Because this seating area is where the family spends the most time, it was important for it to be cozy, inviting, and practical, with a comfortable sofa and a sturdy stone-topped table.

LEFT: The primary bedroom is a serene envelope of gunmetal gray; we upholstered the wall behind the bed, and the carpet was woven in the tone of the stained-wood floors for a sense of continuity. An overscale silver-leafed mirror leans against the wall facing the window to bounce light back into the room. ABOVE: My clients already owned the vintage Murano-glass chandelier, which provides a soft glow in the evening; a curvaceous Trudi sofa and Thom chair from VW Home are grouped in front of the windows. The shades were crafted of raw silk by Jim Thompson, and the upholstered storage ottoman at the foot of the bed was custom made.

113

RIGHT: Silver-metallic accents add glints of shimmer to the earthy cork wall covering that clads one side of the top-floor media room; I like the contrast of textures as they mix with Kuba-cloth pillows and a graphic Chinese window. A sumptuous sofa extends across the full depth of the space, providing ample seating to view the flat screen. As shown reflected in the mirror, the screen is displayed on a tubular stand so that it appears to float in front of the curtained stairwell.

Design Integrations

Working with art-collector clients presents both a delightful opportunity and a challenge. Over the years, as I've integrated everything from children's drawings to extraordinary works of art into their homes, I've learned the importance of finding the correct balance—of designing interiors that celebrate and support a collection without creating a distraction. Art should never literally match an interior or vice versa, but furnishings can speak the same language as paintings, sculptures, and photography. Art, whether humble or grand, reflects spirit and emotion, qualities that can transform even the most beautifully designed room into a place with true meaning and soul.

Traditional Values

I have never paid much attention to so-called "rules of decorating"—especially the one that advises you always to design a room around the rug. That being said, the signature color palette of this entire project was, in fact, inspired by an antique Tabriz I had purchased for the home my longtime clients were living in when they embarked on a five-year restoration of a new house, a ramshackle, turn-of-the-century mansion.

The couple, who live in Old Westbury, New York, with their children, had long admired the stately white-brick house surrounded by seven rolling acres not far from their then-home. They would fantasize about making it their own and eventually bought it, although it had been abandoned for over a decade and was in a state of abject disrepair.

Built in 1897, the Georgian-style structure was a magnificent yet formidable challenge. It's funny, people often say, "It needed *everything*," but this place truly did. It not only needed a new roof and central air, but it had to be rewired, replumbed, and completely reconceived. I was my clients' first call; three weeks later, demolition started.

The centerpiece of the house was an extraordinary curved staircase in the entrance gallery—sadly, the elegance ended there. As the house had been renovated over time, with rooms added and others chopped up, it evolved into a rambling warren of small rooms. Along the way, it had lost its personality and its grandeur.

I am very much inspired by David Hicks—the British designer who revolutionized interiors of the 1960s and '70s, modernizing classic, often historic homes without altering their sense of tradition. I soon realized that a restoration wouldn't suffice in this situation; it desperately needed an intervention. We basically took the house down to its shell, hoping to recreate as much of its original splendor as possible.

I reconceived the first floor with an open center hallway stretching the entire length of the structure. We built an addition that comprises a solarium on the first floor and a primary bedroom suite upstairs, and at the opposite end of the long hall we created a breakfast room, enlarged the kitchen, and added a den.

I waited until the construction process was well underway before I presented my plans for the interiors; I wanted the rooms to have taken shape so my clients could better imagine the completed spaces. They are art collectors, with a range of exceptional, striking works, and it was essential that the architecture, the finishes, and especially the furnishings would complement their art, not compete with it. Though their Tabriz rug might have inspired the color palette, it was my clients' passion and vision that enabled their young family to live in a place they once only dreamed of, a home that reflects both their modern, artful design aesthetic and deep-seated respect for the past.

OPPOSITE: The living room of a circa-1897 Georgian-style house that my clients and I restored and brought back to a new, artful life. The antique Tabriz rug from Doris Leslie Blau inspired the colors used throughout the project, a palette that ranges from gunmetal tones to tan and tobacco—moody colors that were often used by the couturier Charles James.

LEFT: A graceful curved staircase, original to the house, joins the first and second floors and serves as a classic counterpoint to my clients' contemporary art collection; I love how it seems to embrace the Soundsuit sculpture by Nick Cave. The center table, with a polished-steel base and stone top, was custom made, and I found the pair of Victorian tufted armchairs in Paris. **ABOVE:** The restoration involved gutting the turn-of-the-century house down to its shell. I installed traditional herringbone floors throughout, staining them a glossy ebony, and though we removed the ornate millwork and floor and ceiling moldings, we replaced the baseboards in the original rooms of the house and recessed them in the new, more streamlined areas—celebrating the new and the old in a subtle, understated way.

RIGHT: The living room is furnished with a mix of antique, vintage, and contemporary pieces, including a pair of high-backed club chairs that I used to anchor this side of the generously sized space. A Pierre Paulin Ribbon chair and 1940s French armchair mingle with an ottoman upholstered in pale kidskin, and I used Japanese lacquered wedding-gift containers as side tables; Parentesi lamps by Flos are installed beside a painting by Dana Frankfort.

LEFT: A photograph by Luis Gispert and Jeffrey Reed is displayed over the living room fireplace, which was original to the house and is flanked by twin velvet-covered sectionals; the lounge chairs are by Warren Platner for Knoll, and I hung the large mirror over the sofa to reflect the lush views outside the windows.

RIGHT: My clients love to entertain, and their dining room was designed to suit intimate groups and family dinners—or can seat up to 20 people at its two custom-made tables. A tufted-velvet banquette that stretches from wall to wall is grouped with a rectangular table that can be extended, while a round table in the center of the room is ringed by a mix of Hollywood Regency–style and upholstered side chairs. On the wall over the banquette, I created an arrangement of antique mirrors; stainless-steel mirrored panels; and antique and vintage gilded, silver-leafed, and black-painted frames. They are all reflective surfaces, but a mix that includes both art and empty frames. **FOLLOWING PAGES:** Though the majority of the rooms in the house are painted white, I played with color and texture in the library. The room is essentially a camel-color envelope, with walls and carpet in a rich, tawny hue and cove moldings and baseboards painted in a glossy tone to match. I designed a wall treatment using an upholstery fabric cut into squares and applied in a directional grid that resembles parquetry, and the fireplace was clad in a wall-to-wall swath of black granite so its off-center placement would appear less obvious; the photograph over the fireplace is by Thomas Ruff. A pair of bookcases inspired by an iconic Billy Baldwin design for Cole Porter stand in front of frosted-glass panels that allow light to spill into the room from the center hall; they flank a vintage 1960s Lucite console.

LEFT: The kitchen needed to function well for a large group, as my clients spend a great deal of time there with family and friends and the wife is a wonderful cook. For example, the island is especially large, 5 feet by 10 feet, to accommodate serving trays and platters of food. I lined the room with stained-gray oak cabinets in a lime-rubbed finish, and the island is topped with polished Cenia Azul limestone, a matte version of the same stone used for the floor. The stainless-steel Wolf range was placed at the end of the space to serve as a room divider between the kitchen and the den. The sculptural ceiling fixture is an Artemide design, the Bottega counter stools are from Design Within Reach, and the tribal rug is from Doris Leslie Blau; a neon work by Tracey Emin is displayed on the far wall.
ABOVE: A "before" photo shows the kitchen under construction, with the opening leading to the den addition beyond.

BEFORE

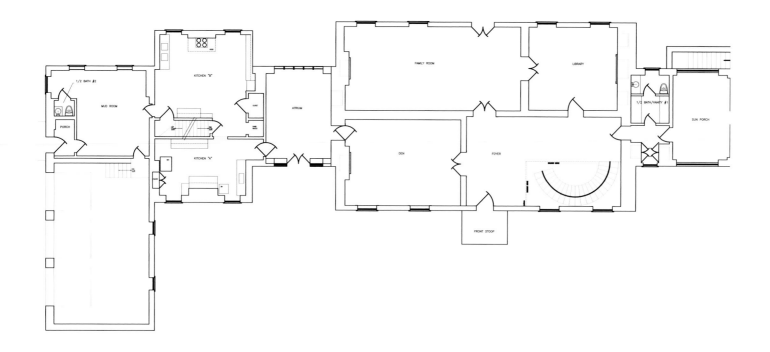

AFTER

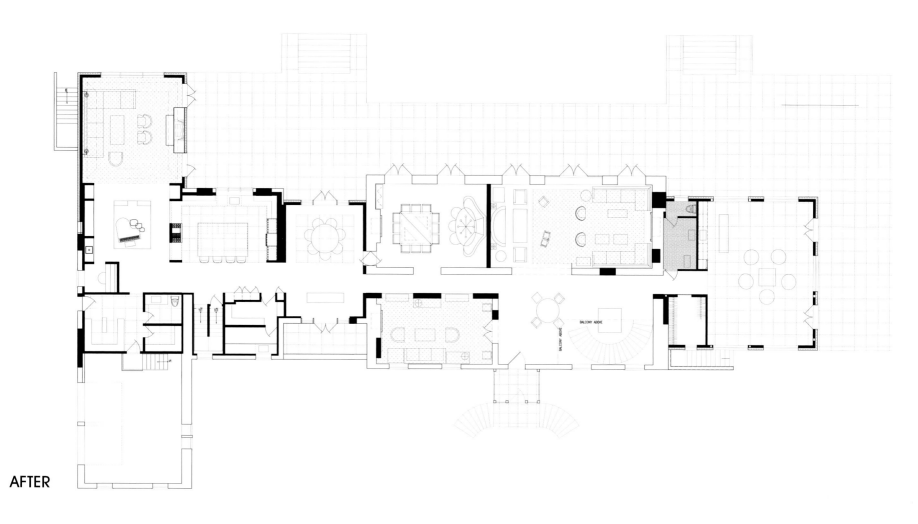

Design Lessons

- When working with art-collecting clients, it's important to be familiar with the works in their collections and where they hope to place them before you start to plan lighting and furniture designs.

- The way art is displayed needs to tell a story. It's not just hanging each piece on a wall—it's what is next to it, and how the work relates to everything else in the room. It's important to understand the vision behind a particular collection, the threads that tie the individual works together.

- When staining floors, always stain the edges of each plank to match the top. This is especially important with dark stains, as wood contracts during cold weather and the lighter edges of the natural wood boards are often revealed.

- In a contemporary space, I like to light a room using recessed ceiling fixtures without any trim— I use square, rimless lights; round fixtures look more traditional to me. And dimmers, always, regardless of the style of a room. Light dimmers can create instant magic.

- If the floor plan can accommodate it, I like to float a bed in the center of a bedroom whenever possible; it's so calming and peaceful to be surrounded by open space.

ABOVE: To smoothly connect the original structure with its additions, we white-washed the brick façade to create a soft, slightly aged patina, and awkward steps that once led from the driveway to the entrance were reoriented to curve around newly landscaped greenery. The entrance now better reflects the scale and grace of the property.

LEFT: The den, a casual space located around the corner from the kitchen, feels separate yet connected because of the open layout. Sculptural seating—Arne Jacobsen's Egg chair for Fritz Hansen and Gaetano Pesce's Up chair by B&B Italia—softens the straight lines of the room and its tray ceiling, and I designed the L-shaped sectional and cowhide-covered ottoman to accommodate a crowd. **ABOVE:** We created an area for my clients' Steinway piano in between the center hall and the den, which includes a room divider fashioned from a 1950s wooden screen from the Czech Republic, and a trio of wool "boulder" cushions crafted by Ronel Jordaan. **FOLLOWING PAGES:** My favorite space in the house is the solarium, a sun-drenched, glass-enclosed room with limestone floors that continue outside to the terrace. Here, a pair of majestic stone sphinxes—antique garden statuary that I discovered in Paris—preside over a fleet of Bonacina's Palla chairs and a vintage Tovaglia molded-fiberglass coffee table from 1stDibs; the cowhide rugs are from Edelman. The bar was custom made with a polished-steel base and a live-edge teak top from Bali, and the woven-leather barstools are from Holly Hunt.

135

ABOVE: The primary suite features his-and-hers bathrooms with gleaming, glamorous finishes. RIGHT: The primary bedroom is cocoonlike, enclosed on three sides with floor-to-ceiling silk curtains, and the bed sits atop a low, sheepskin-covered platform; a gilded Dutch-Colonial cabinet from Indonesia and an 18th-century cardinal's chair add extra drama.

LEFT: In the poolhouse, we installed NanaWall folding-glass doors that open to create a seamless indoor-outdoor space, and the Metropolitan chairs by B&B Italia, covered in Janus et Cie performance fabric, swivel to enable guests to enjoy the view. **ABOVE:** The rear façade of the house reveals the striking juxtaposition of the original structure and its contemporary updates and additions.

In the Spotlight

Photography has been a lifelong interest—not only shooting my own pictures but also, over the years, purchasing from galleries and at auction sales a range of photographs that have moved me in some manner. Not surprisingly, when a long-standing client asked me to design an interior in which he would display a portion of his art collection that was primarily photography, I jumped at the opportunity.

We worked together on several projects via a recommendation from a magazine-editor friend. When the client mentioned that he wanted a new home to be decorated in a Balinese style, the editor promptly responded, "You should meet Vicente Wolf; he travels."

This opportunity, however, wasn't another residence, but rather a business setting in which to host meetings and dinners and to store and display a sizable photography collection, including numerous images by Ansel Adams, the iconic American landscape photographer and environmentalist. The location was also different: an approximately 3,500-square-foot loft in downtown Manhattan. The renovated, former industrial space featured soaring ceilings, a wall of windows, gleaming wood floors, and exposed-brick walls. Though I'm not keen on brick, I could easily envision this as an exclusive private art gallery.

One of our first decisions was to leave the industrial sprinkler system and HVAC ductwork exposed. We painted the sprinkler pipes and ceiling the same bright white, and left the aluminum air ducts that stretch the length of the area raw to provide a strong counterpoint to the muted tones of the brick walls. I like the gutsiness this brings to the room.

Having lived most of my life in a loft, I've found it best to deal with such spaces in an unconventional way—a traditional furniture layout has always seemed out of sync in places that will somehow always feel a bit industrial. Instead, I create settings with a loose, less formal quality to them. To avoid placing sofas up against a wall, I float them, and I put casters on almost all chairs and tables—anything that I might want to move around easily when entertaining.

Here, I created two seating areas, one by the bookshelves, with deep club chairs for reading, and another in front of the stacked-marble fireplace. Objects and artifacts are set atop pedestals, and photographs are displayed individually or in sets of two or four; I wanted there to be a rhythm to them. I added a flotilla of small ceiling lights to illuminate the room and a track of spotlights to focus on individual photographs, while the conference/dining table is lit by a grouping of white pendant lamps that dangle like earrings from swooping cords. And though I'll admit that the sea of brick was a bit daunting at first, with its rugged, earthy quality, it proved to be an exquisite backdrop for a dazzling collection of black-and-white images that celebrate nature at its very best.

OPPOSITE: A vignette in a collector's downtown-Manhattan loft features a wide-ranging assortment of art and artifacts; the monumental bookcase is stacked with objects and art books.

LEFT: My client uses the gallery-like space to host business meetings and to display his striking collections, which include photographs by Ansel Adams, as well as objects, artifacts, and mementos from his travels. I designed a series of plinths and pedestals of different heights and we painted them in black and white to complement the photography and to provide contrast with the earthy tones of the brick walls.

Design Lessons

o I'm a firm believer that a loft is a loft—don't try to turn one into a traditional-style space. It's rarely a good fit.

o Framing a collection in the same color of frame, or in gilded frames, for instance, will create a sense of cohesion, even if the photos or artworks are quite dissimilar.

o When planning a salon-style wall of art, it's best to measure the wall space and tape the area out on the floor, where you can move the pictures around and place them in the most appealing composition. It's easier to experiment on the floor before hammering anything into the wall. Also be sure to use the measuring tape when you mark where to place the hooks—this is not the time to wing it.

o Never frame artwork with glass—always use Plexiglas, which not only helps to filter out harmful UV rays but offers protection from damage if the work happens to fall; it's shatterproof.

o Consider hanging artwork in the traditional style—from ceiling moldings instead of wall hooks. This can be done in a contemporary manner by hanging works with metal wire or heavy-duty monofilament from a rod suspended at the top of the wall; the works look like they're floating, and you have the flexibility to move them around. There are also some well-designed picture-rail systems that are offered in a variety of styles.

ABOVE: A "before" shot of the space, which was a classic, renovated loft with clean brick walls, exposed sprinklers and HVAC, and polished wood floors. RIGHT: When generous space is required for seating, I often use two large dining tables set atop wheels and pushed together as one long surface; they can be separated easily to accommodate an even larger crowd—though it's always important to keep the placement of ceiling lights in mind. Here, I installed a grouping of AIM pendant lamps that were designed by Ronan and Erwan Bouroullec for Flos—I love that they are suspended on deep loops of cords, as the curves soften the lines of the tables and are a nod to the nearby brick arches. The vinyl-covered seating is a mix of side chairs and left- and right-armed chairs that can be placed together as settees. FOLLOWING PAGES: I created two seating areas, one with deep club chairs for reading, and another grouping with an L-shaped sectional sofa in front of a stacked-marble fireplace that had been installed during the renovation; an Ansel Adams photograph is displayed on a vintage artist's easel.

Language Lessons

There aren't many clients who will say to me, "Make it exciting. Blow me away. Give me WOW!" But the clients who live in this artful Manhattan apartment often do—and I love them for it. Great art collectors with no restrictions, they are open to everything and drawn to quirky pieces, wonderful objects, a mix of old and new.

The couple originally owned only part of their present apartment, which is located on Central Park West and boasts spectacular views of the park; I had designed the interiors for them in a neutral palette and a style *Elle Decor* described as "urban Zen." Several years later, when they purchased the place next door, they commissioned me to combine the two, though with a refreshed design aesthetic. Their home now showcases brighter color, a wider range of their art collection, and an exuberant, more freewheeling personality.

They use this residence as a pied-à-terre; their primary home is on Long Island, and this is a place they come to stay for a weekend or overnight after going to the opera. The husband requested a room where he could relax and watch television, while the wife wanted a space where they could entertain—though usually just drinks with friends before seeing a performance. In fact, when planning the renovation, they decided to forgo a formal dining room in favor of an intimate dining area with a park view.

In my experience, conjoined apartments offer enormous opportunity in addition to the inherent challenges of unifying the space. My decision to open a few strategic walls made the main living area feel loftlike, yet designed with different seating areas to suit their needs. Forced to work around structural beams, heating and plumbing risers, and fireplace flues, to help unify the space we painted the walls a pristine matte white, with the ceilings in a high-gloss finish to reflect the sky and trees just beyond the windows.

The design brief was clear: The wife loved anything unconventional, which greatly appealed to me. They have a substantial art collection, and she wanted striking furnishings that would serve as exclamation points in the space, providing a strong counterbalance to their distinctive works. My goal was to find furniture pieces that had some friction between them, yet also a sense of cohesion. Everything came together in an idiosyncratic mix of pieces they owned—like a Surrealist bird-legged Meret Oppenheim table—and those that I found, including a quirky Venetian Art Deco pendant lamp that I hung next to their bed.

I've always appreciated how important it is not only to listen and pay attention to clients' needs but to also learn to speak their language. My clients' collection reflects very clearly who they are, and we created an environment that, in addition to fulfilling practical needs, truly celebrates their passion. These interiors were not designed around their collection; instead, the architecture, the furnishings, and the art seamlessly speak as one.

OPPOSITE: In an art-filled apartment high above New York City's Central Park, a sapphire-blue Vladimir Kagan sofa from Holly Hunt is grouped with a banker's chair wrapped in gold tape by artist Rob Pruitt, a midcentury tea-height table with a polished-steel base, and a vintage Pedro Friedeberg Hand chair; the sculpture behind the sofa is by Walead Beshty.

LEFT: We removed the wall between the living room and den to create an open living area. The sofas are upholstered in a deep-blue mohair, which feels very French to me, and I custom designed the steel-and-glass cocktail table; the acrylic Jonquil chair is by Erwine and Estelle Laverne—in a playful move, I had the carpet cut to follow the silhouette of its circular base. ABOVE: The piece that best reflects my clients' embrace of the unexpected is an 18th-century Italian Rococo console table that serves as a sort of room divider. Likely once gilded, it was raw wood when I found it, with a marble top that we replaced with a slab of bright-orange resin and bisected with a steel tube that displays an artwork on one side and a flat screen on the reverse. The Brillo-box sculpture near the window is by Andy Warhol; we installed blackout shades behind linen Roman shades throughout the apartment to protect the art collection when my clients are away.

LEFT: For a far corner of the living area, I designed a settee with a slightly curved frame; it's fully upholstered, including its legs, in a marine-blue cotton blend with a wide border treatment. The armchair is by Warren Platner for Knoll, and the table is a vintage design by Meret Oppenheim; I loved the idea of this table that looks like a standing bird juxtaposed with birds flying from tree to tree outside the windows.

ABOVE, FROM TOP: The room we call the gallery offers beautiful park views; at right, a contemporary triptych by Richmond Burton is placed on an antique library stand. In the center of the room, a painted-wood sculpture by Robert Gober is on display, and the far wall features a niche with glass shelves we designed to showcase the wife's collection of Murano-glass animals produced by Italian glass masters. RIGHT: I like the contrast of the antique gilded mirror and the crisp minimalism of the fireplace surround, which is flanked by a series of screenprints by Adam Pendleton; the sculptures of figures are by Daniel Oates.

your kiss
on the skin
of my
soul

i wanted
justice
under
my
nose

nobody
nobody
cold

BEFORE

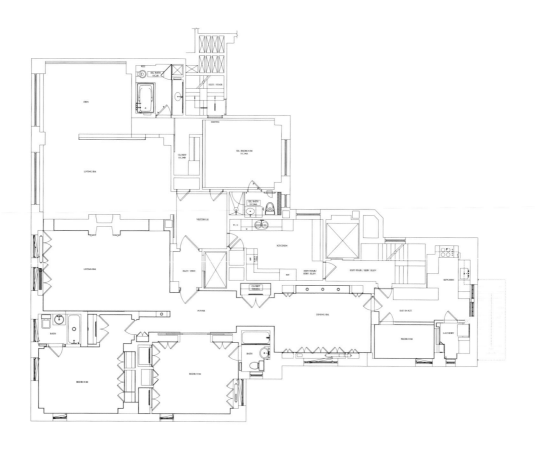

AFTER

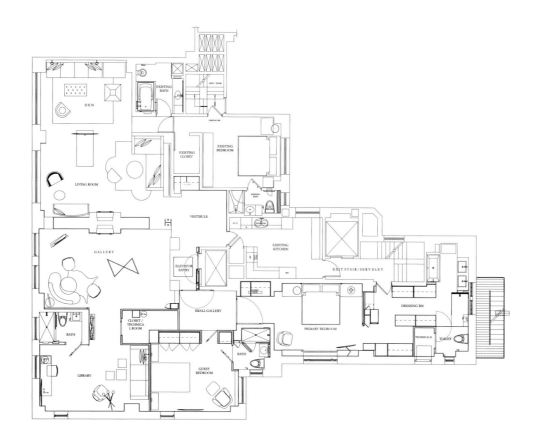

Design Lessons

○ Sunlight and UV rays can be damaging to artwork, not to mention upholstery and carpets, so we often create a pocket in the ceiling above a window in which to conceal a blackout shade behind curtains or a Roman shade. This is especially important for residences that are in use only part-time.

○ I like the effect of a high-gloss paint finish; it not only creates instant glamour, but when used on a ceiling, it can make a room seem taller, and on both ceilings and walls, it can reflect a beautiful view. However, always be conscious of what might be reflected if using a lacquer or glossy finish—sometimes reflections can obscure the gleaming surface, and sometimes there are things that should remain unseen.

○ Don't be hesitant to replace the top of a traditional table or chest to make it look more contemporary—try using frosted glass or colored resin for a totally new look. And, if possible, be sure to save the original top for use elsewhere.

○ I often remove walls to create a big open space, or I might create small seating areas within a larger area—and at times I do both, as I did in this apartment. There aren't any strict rules to follow—just your intuition as to how the space will look and work best.

○ I'm always drawn to furniture, objects, lighting, and rugs that are sculptural, as they can add unexpected poetry to a space.

LEFT: In the library, a wood-veneer wall covering in a warm taupe hue serves as a muted background for works by Torben Giehler, at left, and Cindy Sherman; I designed the sofa to be upholstered in Edelman cowhide with cushions in a polished wool from VW Home. The room's color palette was inspired by a textile I bought on a trip to Papua New Guinea that I used to make pillows I paired with teal-blue cushions on the sofa; the 18th-century Italian chair is covered in robin's egg–blue leather, an unexpected combination that I knew would please my client. **ABOVE:** A John Chamberlain sculpture is displayed on a platform at the entrance to the library.

161

ABOVE: The primary bath is located in space that was formerly the kitchen. It is clad in a beautiful Palissandro Nuvolato marble from Italy, and I found a tall Syrian mother-of-pearl–inlaid chest to provide extra storage. RIGHT: In the primary bedroom, we placed the bed to face a window that has a view of the dome of a neighborhood church. Both the bed and headboard are upholstered, and I installed subtle lighting to illuminate the Bruce Boyce works displayed over the headboard. One of my favorite finds is a quirky Venetian Art Deco pendant light that hangs over the nightstand at right.

Artistic License

I've been fortunate that my design practice has always balanced an exciting mix of new clients along with those who are long-standing. Over the years, many have become close friends, and I've found the majority to be reasonably consistent in their tastes and aesthetics—every once in a while, however, they can throw me for a loop.

This was the case with a couple for whom I'd designed four projects, including a classic Park Avenue prewar apartment and a Shingle-style house in the Hamptons. Though they have a dazzling collection of contemporary art that they've assembled over the years, their design preferences always trended toward the classic, even traditional. (I'm so fond of them, I actually once agreed to upholster a sofa in a vibrant floral chintz at the request of the wife.)

They decided to sell their house near the ocean in favor of moving to a renovated 19th-century factory building in a charming bayside village not far away. When choosing between two of the spacious condo apartments, the husband asked which I would select—one was rather square and symmetrical while the other was oddly shaped, with a quirky curved extension at one end. Finding the curved space awkward, I opted for symmetry, but my client disagreed and chose the less predictable of the two.

The couple was drawn to the gutsy, raw feeling of the loft, which had been renovated with every imaginable modern convenience while retaining exposed-brick walls, wide-plank floors, and beamed timber ceilings. It also boasted beautiful treetop and harbor views. The husband wanted this strikingly different new home to be both artful and surprising, showcasing an exhilarating new expression of their collection.

After studying the layout, I designed around its challenges, treating the rounded space as an alcove and anchoring it with a curved sofa to follow the shape of the room. I proposed painting the brick white and sandblasting it to lend a timeworn patina. Though the couple were initially apprehensive, once the painting began they saw how it unified the space, providing a stronger, more distinctive background for their paintings and sculpture.

The wife chose a color palette of soft greens and blues, which I loved; interestingly, not one piece of furniture ended up in the same fabric—they were all in similar hues, but in a mix of linen, leather, and polished wool textiles. The sculptural seating serves as a foil to the couple's dramatic, colorful canvases—the chairs, from the 1940s and '60s to 18th-century French and Swedish, are an eclectic group that seemed like a sea of misfits on paper but mingled peacefully when they came together.

It was a delight not only to design this unexpected interior for my friends, but also to thoughtfully place works I admire—including those by Damien Hirst, Ugo Rondinone, and El Anatsui. In truth, now one of my favorites, this project seems less of a surprise every day.

OPPOSITE: In a historic beachside village, this loft apartment in a former factory building features an eclectic mix of periods and styles, including, from left, a midcentury French chair, upholstered steel chaise longue of my design, vintage Danish nesting tables, and an antique Swedish klismos chair. The spin painting is by Damien Hirst.

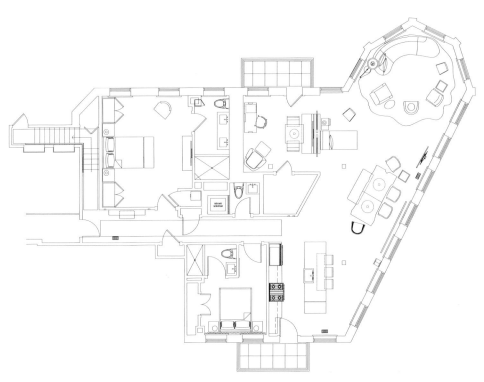

LEFT: The circa-1881 industrial space had been restored and renovated, preserving its original brick walls and exposed beams and ceiling. We left the wood beams raw while painting the timber ceiling white; the walls were also painted white, then sandblasted to create a soft, aged patina. The rounded extension of the main living area would serve as an alcove with a separate seating area. **ABOVE:** A "before" photo of the alcove prior to painting. My floor plan for the spacious yet oddly shaped layout.

Design Lessons

◦ Never match fabrics to the artwork—art shouldn't be relegated to mere decoration; it stands on its own. Most important, an artwork reflects the personal taste of your client.

◦ Free-form rugs make a structured room feel less rigid. They can also prompt you to rethink the traffic flow in a space.

◦ I strive to avoid the expected pattern of a sofa and a pair of club chairs whenever possible. Different seats are comfortable for different people and there are myriad options—upright, slouchy, deep, or shallow; chairs where you might curl up, and others clearly intended for perching. Keep an open mind and consider expanding your choices to include chaise longues and daybeds, stools and benches, slipper chairs and settees.

◦ Don't be intimidated by mounting sleek track lighting onto rustic wood ceiling beams as we did in the loft. I like the juxtaposition of traditional and contemporary, and you can avoid opening the ceiling to install the electrical wiring.

◦ I often use a single color throughout a bedroom—from the upholstered walls to furnishings and lush carpeting. I like my clients to feel protected, as if they're enveloped in a cocoon of tranquility. There is a seductive quality to the luxury of quiet.

LEFT: The living area is flooded with light from oversize windows; I installed sheer-linen Roman shades so the original arched lintels over the windows would remain visible. The hammered-copper cocktail table is a custom design, as is the curved sofa covered in a pale-green Pierre Frey fabric. The seating is a mix of materials and provenance, including, from left, Erwine and Estelle Laverne's 1960s acrylic Jonquil chair; a midcentury René Prou metal armchair, one of a pair; an 18th-century Venetian painted armchair upholstered in Edelman leather; and a linen-upholstered Bridgewater chair. I sketched a free-form rug to suit this unusually shaped space; Dualoy Leather made a paper pattern that we tested on-site before crafting a rug of sheared lambswool. The sculpture atop the pedestal is by Michael Queenland.

RIGHT: In the dining area, a monumental El Anatsui sculpture woven of recycled aluminum fragments and copper wire was installed in front of windows that illuminate it during the day; in the evening it shimmers with reflected light. A Platner armchair and Eero Saarinen's Tulip chairs, all by Knoll, are grouped around a live-edge slab table; the rattan bench by Bielecky Brothers is upholstered in Edelman leather.

LEFT AND ABOVE: A striking Ugo Rondinone painting stretches across the far wall of the office, a room I conceived for both work and play. The Saarinen Womb chair is by Knoll, and the desk is a custom design I had crafted of steel with a thick glass top. My clients like to play cards at the stone-topped table; the Hans Wegner Wishbone chair is a vintage design.

ABOVE AND RIGHT: The primary bedroom is a luminous envelope of pale green with walls covered in a hand-painted silk custom made by Fromental; its soft brushstrokes glimmer with random glints of metallic silver. The upholstered bed is flanked by vintage pendant lights by Foscarini and VW Home stone-topped shagreen nightstands; the bed linens are by Matouk. Extra storage was needed, so I designed these two tall cabinets with doors inlaid in a grid pattern of limed and natural oak. The slipper chair is a favorite vintage design by William Haines, whose work inspired this room; the painting is by Josh Smith.

LEFT: The four-poster in the guest room is by Room & Board; the curtains are of a VW Home fabric hand-painted by Philippe David. ABOVE: Planters of lush hydrangeas border the spacious deck, which is furnished with iconic designs by Richard Schultz for Knoll.

Design Reinventions

As much as I love designing interiors—the entire process from walk-through to conception, presentation, and installation—I love renovations even more. I find it unbelievably exhilarating to see walls coming down, rooms taking shape, and my creative ideas becoming a reality. Perhaps my visual acuity became stronger and more developed as a result of my dyslexia, but I've always had the ability to imagine how a space could be transformed even when there is little evidence of opportunity. Never one to linger on the depressing specifics of a total gut job, I prefer the brilliant promise that a floor plan, a pencil, and a piece of tracing paper can provide, as the possibilities are endless.

A Clean Sweep

Not long after I had finished a house in Westchester for a young family, they approached me with a design dilemma. For several years they had owned a second home in the Hamptons that was built as a "spec house," a Dutch Colonial they now felt they had outgrown—not just its size, but also its aesthetics. Though the couple loved the property, they were undecided whether to look for a new house or to try to fix the current one.

Their situation was hardly surprising—even luxury spec houses are at best convenient and conventional, their compartmentalized spaces laden with design clichés developers employ to appeal to a wide audience. With their ubiquitous overscale fireplaces, elaborate moldings, flashy plumbing fittings, and tricky tilework, most designers find them cringeworthy. To me, they're a feast of fixables.

The construction of an addition to accommodate extra living space and guest rooms was quickly set in motion, and then I essentially took an eraser to the existing floor plan, reconceiving the ground floor as loftlike, a multifunctional layout with areas that flowed from one to the next. Walls and doorways separating the foyer, living room, den, dining room, and kitchen were opened, and the headers and moldings were eliminated; the wood studs were replaced by steel I-beams powder-coated white, adding a clean, architectural element to the space. The sliding glass doors were updated to versions without muntins, and the massive, traditional-style mantel was removed in favor of a smooth fireplace wall with a flat-screen TV; a piece of timber painted glossy white serves as a minimalist mantel ledge.

The most significant transformation was just inside the front door, where I abolished the poky, humdrum vestibule and Sheetrock stairwell, enclosing the steps to the second floor with a luminescent panel of frosted glass and a sheet of tempered glass—surfaces that seemingly float and create a new, modern, Zen-like tone for the entire house.

The mood is consistently casual throughout the first floor; low-slung upholstery in easy-care fabric reflects the soft hues of the beach and sky, and windows are dressed in simple Roman shades or elegant pinch-pleat curtains of sheer cream linen. For flexibility when entertaining, I used the same mix of dining chairs in the breakfast area and dining room—sculptural white chairs that stand up to wet bathing suits and are easily moved.

When the renovation began to progress, I asked my clients to limit their site visits. This sounds somewhat controlling—which is not untrue—though I think they knew it was important for them to experience a revolution instead of incremental changes. And after living in their reimagined house for a while, they told me that I had transformed the way the house not only feels but works—it was the house they always wanted, it just needed to evolve.

OPPOSITE: In an open-plan living area in a Hamptons beach house, I used an antique Indonesian table and a pair of Web Collection armchairs from VW Home to create a sense of separation between the entrance and the living room. The sculptural Castore table lamp is by Artemide.

LEFT: I designed the L-shaped sectional sofa in the living room with cushions covered in two contrasting tones of Janus et Cie fabric. The Parentesi lamps by Flos stretch from floor to ceiling, and the side table is from a collection I designed for RH/Restoration Hardware. The wool "boulder" floor cushions, made by South African artisan Ronel Jordaan, can be used for extra seating.

LEFT: The "before" version of the living room reveals the original stair hall at the far end of the space. BELOW: The revised layout reflects the elimination of multiple walls, doors and headers, and an overscale mantel. The first floor is now one unified space, with multipurpose areas flowing from one to another. OPPOSITE: The first-floor plan, both before and after the renovation.

BEFORE

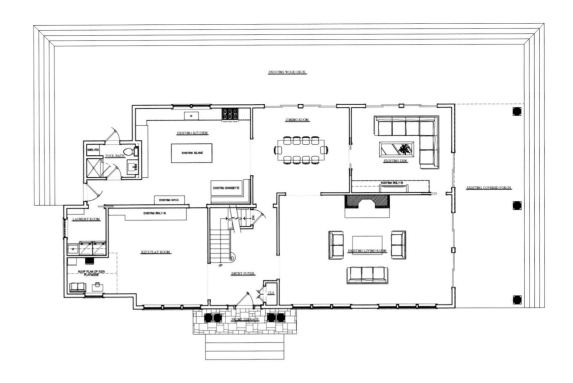

AFTER

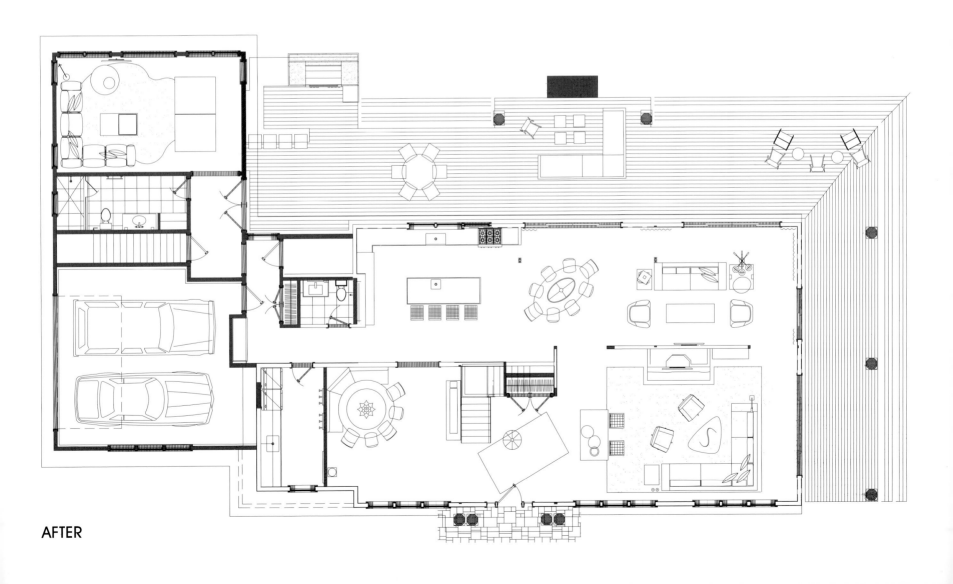

Design Lessons

○ Reimagining a boring staircase can dramatically transform an interior.

○ Hanging an overscale chandelier over a round table that floats in a room will give it presence and create a sense of space even without walls.

○ Unify disparate spaces with curtains and shades in the same fabric and floors and carpet in a similar hue.

○ I sometimes craft tables using a 1¼- to 2-inch-thick slab of glass on a polished-steel base. It's interesting to see a material that is so fragile become something so solid and strong.

○ I love swivel chairs—they allow people to talk to each other without straining—and ottomans, as nothing says "relax" to me more than a place to rest your feet.

○ A boomerang-shaped cocktail table is the perfect complement to an L-shaped sectional sofa. The combination of forms allows for both large and small groups.

○ When I need to create different spaces within a big open room, architectural elements or furnishings can help to define specific areas—for instance, a bookcase or decorative screen or a change in flooring material or carpet. In this house, I used a pair of woven armchairs with a table and vignette of objects to delineate the opening to the living room. The setting draws the eye and acts like a punctuation mark.

RIGHT: The Sheetrock walls of the foyer and stair hall were removed, and the stairs are now an ethereal path bordered by panels of clear and frosted glass. The dining room features a corner banquette and a grouping of Verner Panton chairs by Vitra and Saarinen Tulip chairs by Knoll. The floors throughout this level are stained a soft gray inspired by a piece of driftwood I found on the beach.

LEFT: In the den, the sofa was designed with deep seat cushions and wide arms; a cushioned Web Collection bench from VW Home serves as the cocktail table, the Metropolitan swivel chairs are by B&B Italia, and the cowhide rug is by Edelman. The side table is crafted of a 2-inch-thick slab of glass atop a polished-steel base; I love the light reflected by the vintage beach lanterns that I mounted on metal stands. The wall between the den and former dining room was removed to create a space that now serves as the breakfast area; the wood studs were replaced with steel I-beams painted white.

RIGHT: The Tulip dining table in the breakfast area is an Eero Saarinen design by Knoll and the Halo Circle ceiling lamp is by Roll & Hill. I used a mix of the same sculptural chairs here as in the dining room, so they are interchangeable and provide greater flexibility when my clients entertain. **FOLLOWING PAGES**: I updated the pool area with a sybaritic shaded daybed by Gandia Blasco and chaise longues from CB2.

Small Pleasures

I've always believed that scale and budget have less to do with making a place fabulous than one would think. I love a big project, but I also often find great pleasure in small-scale opportunities—especially those that involve the challenge of reinvention.

This was the case with a Palm Beach apartment purchased about a decade ago by a New York City–based couple with whom I have worked for many years. The husband was eager to escape wintry weather in a warm place where he could play golf and spend time with friends; the wife was amenable but decidedly less enthused.

They found a condo on the Intracoastal Waterway in an elegant 1920s building that was formerly a hotel. With two bedrooms, a galley kitchen, and a convertible den/third bedroom, it was a perfect getaway for them, and one with enough room for visiting family. They opted to buy some of the seller's furniture and then asked me to freshen the decor and help them pull the place together.

Our changes were all surface improvements—fresh paint, slipcovers, new carpet, cosmetic kitchen and bath updates—and some furnishings to fill out the space. They felt the redo was sufficient for a pied-à-terre. As time passed, however, both grew to love being in Palm Beach and eventually came to feel they should either find a new place or make this one better reflect their taste and style.

After a long search, they remained, preferring the apartment's location and water-front views to those of the alternatives. My design brief focused on the main living/dining area and the den—which the couple wanted to feel brighter and more spacious—as well as integrating the enclosed kitchen into the layout. They wanted the overall vibe to be more cohesive, with furnishings that reflected how the space was actually used.

I think the best way to enhance a small space is to give it air. I eliminated the walls and bookcases that closed off the den—what is now the living room—and after the common wall was opened, the kitchen entrance was relocated to the living area; this also created room for a counter and stools and flooded the space with sunlight.

The dining table and chairs now nestle into one corner with a sumptuous curved banquette. A palatial circular sofa commandeers another corner with an ottoman and mix of sleek chairs. The seating and dining areas are separated by ethereal frosted-glass sliding doors that close for privacy (a section of the sofa unfolds into a bed) but otherwise remain open, tucked behind bookshelves and a floating flat-screen TV.

My clients were incredulous that the space could look and feel so different. Transformed from mundane to marvelous, it was replete with a new emotion that reflects the lightness and joy the couple feels here. And what could be more fabulous than that?

OPPOSITE: The dining area of a Palm Beach condo that I reconfigured to visually amplify its square footage. Within a span of six months, we had transformed a rather conventional apartment into a jewel-box space with gleaming surfaces that glow with reflected sunlight.

LEFT: The walls that separated the den from the main living/dining area were removed in favor of sliding frosted-glass doors; the backless bookshelves and translucent glass doors now allow sunlight to flood both parts of the room. The center floor space was left airy and open, and the carpeting was replaced with overscale Glassos tiles installed on a diagonal; this visually expands the space and creates a fresher look for a waterfront home. The dining table and chairs are by Eero Saarinen for Knoll, and the black-and-white photograph is an iconic image by Melvin Sokolsky.

RIGHT: An ottoman, a pair of Thom chairs from VW Home, and a 1940s French armchair are grouped around the capacious sectional sofa in the sitting area, which can accommodate a crowd comfortably. The cabinet installed in the corner showcases a carved Cambodian torso and an 18th-century column capital serves as a side table, displaying an African necklace that I found on my travels. The curved lines of the sofa and the wool-and-jute rug soften the boxy, angular quality of the room.

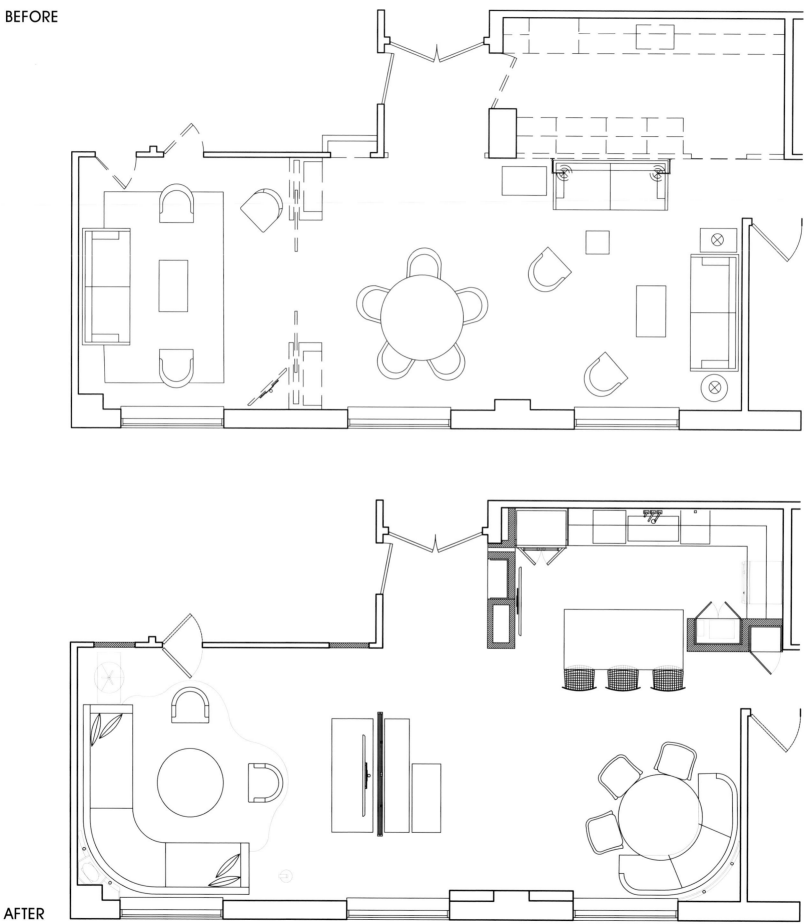

BEFORE

AFTER

Design Lessons

○ Awkward structural juts are ubiquitous in older apartments. Built to accommodate risers, they can create annoyingly uneven sight lines within a room. Whenever possible—and when the loss of floor space is minimal—we fill the space around a jut to create a more unified, elegant look. As an example, in this apartment, a 20-inch-long protrusion between the windows was built out to create an expanded, smooth wall surface on which to display a striking black-and-white photograph.

○ I prefer curved sofas to those with right angles because sitting in the corner is always uncomfortable. A curved sofa is more welcoming—and when grouped with a few chairs and a table or ottoman, its shape encourages people to gather and linger.

○ A useful trick to visually expand a space is to use overscale floor tiles laid on a diagonal. Here, instead of a standard 12-inch size, we installed 4-foot-square Glassos tiles. With fewer seams, they create the sense that the living area is much larger than it is.

○ Topping a windowsill with a thin slab of white marble or glass tile is a subtle move that adds an extra layer of both luxury and practicality.

○ A sofa bed is a wonderful addition to a furnishings scheme. An extra place to sleep is always useful, especially when dealing with modestly sized apartments or vacation homes. It's best to have it custom made by your upholsterer to ensure that it sleeps as well as it sits, and be sure to put any nearby tables on casters to move aside for easy access.

○ Always recess the tracks for sliding doors—whether solid wood or glass—into the ceiling for a seamless, more architectural look.

○ An amoeba-shaped rug adds a sense of playfulness to a space, especially a boxy, linear room. The juxtaposition between the straight and curved geometries is always intriguing.

LEFT: The metal tracks of the frosted-glass doors were embedded into the ceiling for a cleaner line, and we installed a floating flat-screen TV on a metal pole mounted through a marble-topped French 1940s wooden table. **FOLLOWING PAGES:** Opening the galley kitchen to the living/dining area made an enormous difference. The entrance from the foyer was sealed and the common wall removed to make room for a counter faced in stainless steel and a trio of Bertoia counter stools by Knoll. My clients wanted to keep the envelope of white floors and walls as clean-lined as possible, choosing to display only a few meaningful works from their art collection; the lithograph that hangs in the hall leading to the bedrooms is by Alex Katz.

Open House

What do you do when brand-new clients commission you to transform a recent real estate purchase into a contemporary family home—minimalist and ultramodern—even though the property is a late-1970s, classic Shingle-style house brimming with formal moldings, polished dark-wood floors, grilled arched windows, and numerous compartmentalized rooms? The wife could not have been more direct: "I want a glass house."

Reinvention has always appealed to me, and any hesitation about taking on this job was dispelled by its spectacular location: an idyllic Hamptons waterfront property with views of Mecox Bay and the ocean beyond. The house was structured as a rather formal series of rooms leading into one another, with ceilings of varying heights and little connection to the extraordinary grounds. I knew immediately that though the footprint of the house could remain the same, everything else would have to change.

I began by redesigning the ground-floor layout to provide a smooth flow. A long hall serves as an artery behind the main rooms, and I replaced three existing walls with two I-beams to create an open space encompassing a living area and dining area, as well as a family room co-opted from a former porch. The couple entertains frequently, and the individual spaces can be closed off with sliding slatted screens, giving each a personality and function despite the lack of defining walls. It's especially atmospheric by evening candlelight; I love that you can sense the next room without always seeing it.

The bedrooms were updated, the baths and kitchen were renovated, and we installed expanses of glass doors that fold open for a seamless indoor/outdoor experience. We squared off the exterior lines of the house, which we stained a deep, dark slate, while the free-form pool was replaced with a rectangular one reoriented to face the bay.

There's a distinct learning curve when you work with a client for the first time, and an extensive renovation such as this requires not only a generous budget and enormous patience, but also great empathy on the part of the designer. There are constant challenges, including complications that can pop up when you take down a wall, construction delays, late deliveries, and rotten weather; this project definitely had its share.

Following our year-long collaboration, my clients' reinvented home retains the strength and integrity of its original traditional structure while celebrating the openness and light of a modern design. I came to understand that the wife's request for a "glass house" wasn't exactly literal—she wanted that airiness, but her priority was actually a breezy indoor/outdoor family lifestyle. It's a story with a happy ending, as the couple and their children now entertain family and friends and enjoy the pleasures of swimming, tennis, kayaking, and boating all season long in one of the most dazzling settings in the Hamptons.

OPPOSITE: The foyer of a reimagined Hamptons house features an 11½ by 5-foot live-edge slab of wood that I discovered in Bali and had crafted into a distinctive table with a polished-steel base; it provides an earthy quality to the sleek space. The suspension lights are by FontanaArte, and the woven sculpture is by Ghanaian artist Serge Attukwei Clottey.

LEFT: Walls were removed to transform two rooms and a former screened porch into an airy, expansive multipurpose space encompassing living and dining areas and a family room. A pair of I-beams that support the second floor lend an industrial feeling, and NanaWall glass doors that fold completely open were installed to create a seamless interplay between inside and out, amplifying the stunning water views. FOLLOWING PAGES: To maximize space and flow in the main living area, we removed an existing fireplace and surrounding Sheetrock in favor of a frosted-glass wall that allows daylight to spill into the interior hall behind. We faced the glass with slatted screens that are also used elsewhere in the room; the sofa and floating side tables extend from wall to wall, and the sconces are from Louis Poulsen. I designed the leather ottoman and pair of glass-topped steel tables, and the 1950s Cantilever armchairs are by Miroslav Navrátil.

BEFORE

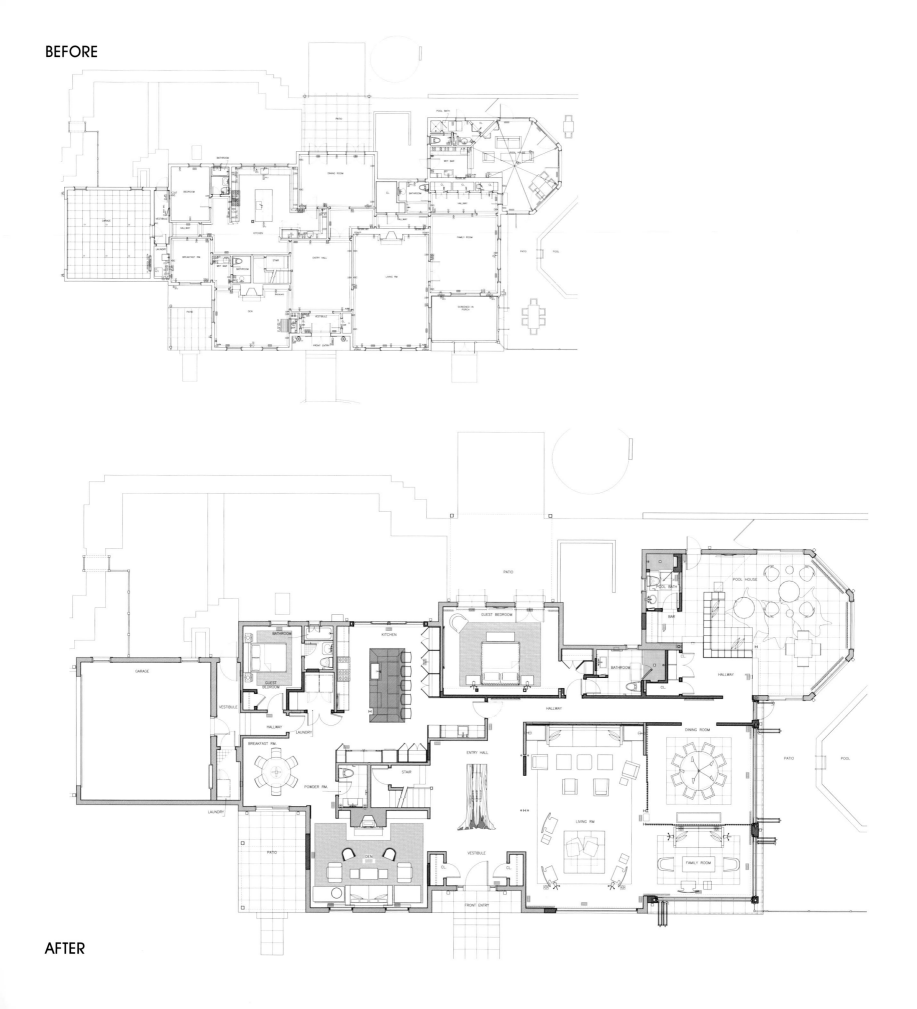

AFTER

OPPOSITE: Before and after plans for the ground floor. **RIGHT:** A "before" photo taken when the family was camping out in the house for the summer season prior to the renovation. **BELOW:** The wall between the entrance hall and living room was replaced with a supporting I-beam, which is illuminated by small spotlights embedded in the floor. **FOLLOWING PAGES:** In the dining room, at left, a table with a satin-nickel base and Glassos top can seat up to a dozen guests comfortably. The Yee chairs are from VW Home, and the Spider chandelier is by Serge Mouille. At right, the family room was formerly a porch. Both rooms open to the terrace via accordion-folding NanaWall doors; to emphasize the inside/outside nature of the layout, I used the same stone tile from the terrace for the interior floors, creating an inset tile square and rectangle, respectively, in the dining area and family room.

Design Lessons

○ I often use sheer fabrics at the window because I like seeing an outside view but appreciate the privacy of a window covering; there's a certain romance to a veiled view. I love the pale shadow grids of sunlight cast through the frame of a window. And never underestimate the value of blackout shades.

○ Not every seating area must consist of a sofa and chairs. I often group four chairs around an ottoman or a cocktail table; the arrangement fosters more intimate, relaxed conversations.

○ When I'm conceiving of a space, I anticipate what it might be like throughout the day and evening. Windows are an important consideration, as they can drench a room with sunlight but turn dark and gloomy once the sun goes down. Well-designed window coverings and effective lighting can help to mitigate any concerns.

○ There's nothing so fresh as a crisp white bathroom. I like to create an envelope of gleaming white surfaces that are softened by stacks of lush white towels.

○ I use reflective surfaces to alter the sense of architecture in a space; large mirrors or sheets of polished steel are elements that are more architectural than decorative.

○ Sliding glass doors are wonderful, but I really love walls of glass that disappear—either gliding into pockets or folding with accordion hinges. With the more casual way we live now, a seamless connection between the interior and exterior has become essential. And there's something particularly wonderful about walking outside without having to pass through a doorway.

○ When it comes to landscape design, it's important to consider the view from the inside out in addition to the exterior vistas—especially, for instance, when planning a parking court or camouflaging the mechanicals of a house. A house should be experienced as beautifully from the interior as from the landscape.

LEFT: I love how the family room's curtains softly billow in the breeze. The curtains are of a Janus et Cie sheer fabric, the Metropolitan chairs are by B&B Italia, and the sofa and Glassos cocktail table are custom designs.

RIGHT: We installed a monumental window in the living area to honor its breathtaking vista of water and sky; it resembles a framed painting. I designed the tufted ottoman as a spot for contemplation; the near section of it is hinged and can be raised to serve as a seat back. The pair of Amalfi chairs was designed by Patrick Naggar for Ralph Pucci, the floor lamps are by Louis Poulsen, and the I Beam side tables are by Ward Bennett for Herman Miller.

OPPOSITE: The den is the only space in the house where I used saturated color, sheathing its walls in a deep-water-blue grass cloth. With a fireplace and a TV, it's a cozy, comfortable room for the family to gather. The marble cocktail table was custom made, the Platner upholstered metal chair is by Knoll, and the lounge chair and ottoman are vintage designs by HBF. I found the ornamental wood fragment that is perched behind the sofa on a trip to Papua New Guinea, and the table lamp is a design by Achille and Pier Giacomo Castiglioni for Flos. Schoolhouse window shades were installed to close from the bottom up to camouflage the parking court visible through the window. ABOVE: A wooden post from Africa is displayed alongside an antique bull's horn.

RIGHT: An octagonal room a few steps down from the living/dining area leads to the pool and serves as the pool-house, though we refer to it as the surfboard room, as I suspended a group of boards from the ceiling. With its low, deep sectional sofa and a small kitchen and bath, it's a no-fuss place to hang out. The swivel chairs are by B&B Italia, the sofa was custom designed, and I shot the overscale photograph of bamboo while on my travels.

LEFT: The walls of the primary bedroom are painted a soft blue hue, referencing the sky and water views that are visible when lying in bed and reflected in the panel of polished steel installed above. The bed is upholstered, placed against a wainscot of cerused oak with integrated nightstands; the vintage ceramics are from Thailand, the bedding is by Matouk, and the coverlet is made of a silk by Jim Thompson. **ABOVE:** A tufted upholstered mattress tops the window seat; the slipper chairs are vintage, and the Etruscan table is a John Dickinson reproduction from Sutherland.

ABOVE: The primary suite's bathtub and shower are installed in a spacious room that is separated from the rest of the bathroom by glass panels. RIGHT: The bath fittings are sleek and sculptural; I found the antique marble bench in India. FOLLOWING PAGES: We streamlined the silhouette of the house as much as possible, and I like the pleasing interplay between its squared lines and slightly curved roof; the exterior was stained Dark Slate, a striking color by Cabot. The free-form pool was replaced by one in a rectangular shape with an interior painted dark gray; the circular daybeds are by Ramón Esteve for Vondom and the Eclipse cantilevered umbrellas are by CB2.

Design Freedom

I don't believe in the adage, "Do as I say, not as I do." Nearly anything found in my Manhattan loft would fit into one of my design jobs and vice versa, though there are certainly more layers of objects in place here.

My apartment reflects an instinctual approach to design. I have no fear of mixing style, color, period, or provenance. There are pieces that are cutting-edge, and others that are vintage or even ancient, but in this industrial-loft environment, they all look like they belong. Furniture, art, and accessories may come and go, but there are pieces I will always treasure, elements that forge the emotional connection that makes this place my home.

Freedom of Choice

I've long taken to heart something that my friend Twyla Tharp once said: "Standing still is actually moving backward." I strive to continue building on whatever I have done before, and my Manhattan loft reflects this mindset more than anything else. My home is in a constant state of evolution and change.

When it came time for me to break out on my own in the late 1980s, I needed to find a space where I could both live and work. It was important that this new place would truly represent my own aesthetic and point of view, and I had certain criteria: I wanted a loft; it needed to be light and bright; and the monthly rent had to fit my limited budget. The space I found was a former photographer's studio in Hell's Kitchen—a seriously edgy part of the city but one that somehow appealed to me; it was scary but down-to-earth.

The loft was beyond filthy, and its concrete floors were painted an odious shade of Kelly green, but it boasted a wraparound lineup of enormous windows with views to the north, east, and south. I am fortunate to be able to imagine things beyond what I can see in front of me, and the day I scouted the space it was drenched in sunlight despite the layers of muck on the windowpanes. I signed immediately.

I did all the work myself—scrubbing, cleaning, repairing, and painting. In fact, the concrete floors have been repainted bright white on a regular basis for the past three decades, though painters now do the work. At the beginning, the primary role of the space was as an office. In the morning, I would put out desks, and when night fell, they would be folded up and put away for the next day. I worked there for nearly a year until my business grew successful enough to open a separate office, which was conveniently located in another loft just a few buildings to the east.

After seven years, I purchased the loft next door to my one-bedroom apartment; it had a wonderful terrace and views both south and west. That's when the apartment truly began to transform. I opened my former bedroom to the main living area, and it now serves as a guest room/exercise space/TV room. The kitchen in the new space was enlarged and renovated, its bedroom became my library, and the former living room is now a primary suite with a dressing room and spacious bath. A long hall along the wall of southern-facing windows joined the two apartments seamlessly.

The neighborhood has changed dramatically since I moved in. The skyscrapers of Hudson Yards loom nearby and new structures surround me. When a building was built next door at the property line, I lost a wall of windows that faced east; after a brief period of mourning, I installed a wall-to-wall picture ledge in its place and haven't given it another thought, the advantage of short-term memory.

OPPOSITE: Misha, my beloved Maine Coon–mix cat, saunters across the concrete floor of my Manhattan loft. A Paul Outerbridge photo is propped atop an antique French chair upholstered in Edelman leather, the chromogenic print is by Michal Rovner, and the Daphine floor lamp is one that I bought nearly 40 years ago.

PRECEDING PAGES: A 19th-century ironwood daybed from Borneo anchors the main living area; the Saarinen table is vintage, the wool "boulder" cushions are by Ronel Jordaan, and the cowhides are by Edelman. I installed the wall-to-wall picture rail when I had to seal the original windows and Sheetrock the wall due to a new building constructed at the lot line. ABOVE: A leather-covered antique Gainsborough chair is grouped with a 1950s Italian table from 1stDibs; the Buddha is my favorite, as its expression is beautiful. RIGHT: A Bridgewater chair by De Angelis partially obscures a 6-foot-tall Joseph Rivière plaster maquette of a female nude that I purchased at a Paris auction; the painting is by Gary Komarin, and the chair in the foreground is a 19th-century Ethiopian chieftain's chair.

I find that I view my work for clients with a far more critical eye than I do my own home. And though there must be a reason behind every decision I make on a client's behalf, here, there is no rhyme or reason—or perfection, as an industrial loft is almost by definition imperfect. With no rules to follow, I have the freedom to redesign whenever I wish—whether it's when I fall in love with a new painting, or because I'd like to experience the space differently. I'm able to experiment, and something that might start out rather haphazardly here often ends up as an element in a client's designed environment.

The foundation of this loft can be defined by two categories: art, primarily photography, and a few key pieces of furniture that are an integral part of my life. Photography is a great passion, as I love the sense of freezing a moment in time; I can feel the emotion that was happening when an image was captured whenever I look at it. My art collection has expanded to include paintings and sculpture, but the selection of photography very much reflects who I am. And some of the furnishings—including a Maison Jansen lacquer table, a leather Papa Bear chair, an angular Daphine floor lamp, and a beloved antique daybed from Borneo—might move from room to room but I doubt they will ever leave.

There are longtime favorites that often show up in my work as well, like classic Gainsborough and Bridgewater chairs, a Saarinen Tulip table, leather hides as rugs or covering furniture, and Parentesi lamps. I especially love the architectural quality of the Parentesi lamp; it stands free, untethered to a wall, able to work high or low. It's a vertical sculpture of light.

The fabrics I use here are favorites, too—the curtains in the bedroom are of a polished wool from VW Home that I love for its weight and subtle sheen. Mohair is incredibly strong and unbelievably soft. I like the practicality of leather, and the best leathers have a wonderful texture, not too rough and not too smooth. Sheer, gauzy linens are perfect at the window or as bed curtains; tone-on-tone damask is so elegant and the only traditional weave that I like; and indoor/outdoor performance fabrics are now so sophisticated, I use them everywhere.

These are the things that I choose to live with in an ever-changing apartment that is not only a haven but also a place that expands my creative vision. There's not one day, throughout every season and all kinds of weather, that I'm not uplifted and energized by this eclectic, free-ranging space.

Travel never fails to open my eyes, my mind, and my heart, but I'm always happy to return home to this beloved loft. I still get the same joy when I open the door and see sunlight pouring in. The art and furnishings that mingle here are all friends. I treasure the photography I collect and the objects that I might have bought five decades—or five days—ago. I can gaze at them and still discover something new.

Perhaps that's the best way to describe a home: It's a space that when you walk in, you love it; you love what you live with, and it makes you happy to be there. I'm appreciative to have been able to create this for myself—and that emotional sense of home is what I hope my clients feel as well. That's a design lesson that will always ring true.

LEFT: The windows throughout the loft are overscale, each measuring 4½ by 5½ feet. This seating area is adjacent to the former division between my original loft and the apartment that I purchased next door. I covered a 19th-century French settee with a hide to complement the color palette of the main living area; the Stephen chair, at left, and Lipstick chair, on the right, are both by VW Home.

ABOVE: The gilded console table is 19th-century French, with a marvelous marble top. OPPOSITE: I discovered the iron chair, attributed to Gilbert Poillerat, in the Paris flea market. The trompe l'oeil drum table is from a show-house project, as is the slipcovered pouf. The collage on the floor is by John Stezaker, and the photographs on the picture rail are by, from left, Claude Batho, Walker Evans, Iwao Yamawaki, and Baron Adolf de Meyer.

LEFT: The guest room/TV room was originally my bedroom when I bought the loft, and this steel daybed was my first bed. I found the twisted-iron garden table at the Paris flea market many years ago; the Chinese plate is from Vietnam and was recovered from a shipwreck. The Thom chair, at left, is by VW Home; the vintage Papa Bear chair, at right, a Hans Wegner design, was a gift from a friend. A Damien Hirst print is propped on the windowsill behind an early-20th-century monk's table, and, at right, an antique stupa from Thailand is displayed in a niche.

RIGHT: The black-lacquer Maison Jansen dining table in the library can open and extend for a dinner party; it's a classic design that I fell in love with in my 20s on my first trip to Paris and knew I wanted to someday own. A grouping of Buddhist ceremonial seashells is displayed on the table, and all of the images in the setting are of hands. The French and neoclassic Italian chairs were purchased at auction; they are flanked by potted aloe plants, which I love for their rambunctious quality. The light in my loft is perfect for trees and plants—a variety of orchids, jasmine, philodendron, ficus, and more thrive year-round.

Design Lessons

- Every few months, take a fresh eye to your interiors: If something has been in the same place for too long—whether it's a piece of furniture or art—you stop seeing it.

- Streamlined, minimalist interiors can benefit from accessories or furniture pieces that have some texture and warmth to them; anything that lends a sense of earthiness will prevent a space from seeming too austere.

- Picture rails are a mainstay of my design practice. They encourage a more direct and immediate relationship with your art collection, as works can be rearranged easily to highlight a new acquisition, to showcase a piece with particular meaning, or even just to be picked up for a closer look. I love the flexibility they offer, and when painted white against a white wall, they simply disappear.

- My travels, which have taken me literally around the world, have deeply informed my creative mindset. Inlaid pieces are always on my radar, especially when shopping in India, but I've also found some that are Syrian, English, and Portuguese. Artisanal furniture like this, as well as ceramics, ethnic necklaces, and headpieces—anything beautifully handcrafted—can serve as idiosyncratic, signature pieces in an interior. They will catch the eye and remain memorable.

- An exotic orchid is like poetry—or music—in a quiet interior, and topiaries can add a sense of architecture to a room; with their deep green color, they act as punctuation marks.

- I strive for contrast and friction in both my home and my work—old against new, rough against smooth, classic against cutting-edge. My keywords are balance rather than strict symmetry, and juxtaposition rather than uniformity.

LEFT: The photographs in my bedroom include images by Dorothea Lange, Edward Weston, and Edward Steichen. The tufted settee is vintage, the slipcovered chair is by De Angelis, and the Ashanti stool is African; I found the lacquer drum table in Burma.

RIGHT: The bedroom's French doors open to the terrace, which is shaded by wisteria; the floor-to-ceiling curtains are of Colette polished wool from VW Home. I've always loved sleigh beds and upholstered this curvaceous version in mohair. The collage displayed on the easel at left is by Alexandr Rodchenko.

LEFT: The De Angelis chair in my dressing room is upholstered in a Janus et Cie performance fabric. In the adjacent bathroom, an antique Burmese table serves as a vanity with a stainless-steel Kohler sink and fittings. I stow my towels under the sink in a vintage Donald Deskey table.

RIGHT: Though the Hell's Kitchen skyline has changed markedly—and continues to change—my terrace remains a beautiful spot from sunrise through the end of the day. I often host small dinners here, as the evening sky is magical and at night the lights in the tall buildings shimmer like stars.

To great friends and very special people
who have allowed me to shine—all are dear to my heart:

Ninah and Michael Lynne

Beth and Ron Ostrow

Kristin and Dick Tarlow

Virginia and Neil Weiss

Acknowledgments

I believe that my success is largely due to having always been in the right place at the right time, and for this I am very grateful.

This book would not have been possible without the following people, to whom I send my thanks:

To Margaret Russell, a true friend who kindly re-envisioned this project when I was at a loss, giving the book an elegant organization, great heart, and a distinct point of view.

To Marianne Williamson, a friend and client who so generously agreed to write my foreword.

To Charles Miers and Katheen Jayes at Rizzoli, whose great patience and support carried this book to completion.

To Jill Cohen, the best book agent a designer could have.

To Sam Shahid, Matthew Kraus, and John MacConnell of Shahid / Kraus & Company for giving form and shape to my thoughts and designs.

To Andrea Monfried, who got the ball rolling.

To Briana-Cecilia Fulgoni, who jumped in and helped with organization, digitization, and handholding, and to Stacy Mahon, who keeps both the office and my life running smoothly.

To Suzanne Sokolov, who brought her knowledge and expertise to this project.

To the clients whose homes are included in these pages, for trusting my creativity and vision.

To my staff who contributed to these projects, including David Rogal, Natalia Ramirez, John Mistriotis, and the whole team at Vicente Wolf Associates.

To the artisans and suppliers who, through their exquisite craftsmanship, made these interiors possible.

And to Matthew Yee, for his love and support, always.

First published in the United States of America in 2023 by
Rizzoli International Publications, Inc.
300 Park Avenue South
New York, NY 10010
www.rizzoliusa.com

Copyright © 2023 Vicente Wolf
Text: Margaret Russell
Foreword: Marianne Williamson

All photographs by Vicente Wolf except:
Page 9: Photograph by Pieter Estersohn. Reprinted with permission of *Elle Decor* © 1995
Page 10: Clockwise from Left, *Interiors Magazine*, May 1981, Photograph by Bruce Wolf;
top right, *Architectural Digest*, Photograph by Peter Vitale; bottom right, Patino/Wolf Associates
Page 11: Patino/Wolf Associates
Page 13: Top left and right, *New York Times Sunday Magazine*, April 9, 1989, courtesy of *The New York Times*; bottom right, Cover, *Metropolitan Home*, March 1991, Photograph by Jon Jenson, Hearst Magazine Media, Inc.
Page 14: Bottom right, Photography Vicente Wolf for Anichini, image courtesy of Anichini.
Pages 192–3: Tria Giovan Photography

Publisher: Charles Miers
Senior Editor: Kathleen Jayes
Production Manager: Barbara Sadick
Managing Editor: Lynn Scrabis

Designed by Sam Shahid
Art Directed by John MacConnell, Shahid / Kraus & Company

Printed in Singapore

2023 2024 2025 2026 / 10 9 8 7 6 5 4 3 2 1

ISBN: 978-0-8478-7296-1

Library of Congress Control Number: 2022945715

Visit us online:
Facebook.com/RizzoliNewYork
Twitter: @Rizzoli_Books
Instagram.com/RizzoliBooks
Pinterest.com/RizzoliBooks
Youtube.com/user/RizzoliNY
Issuu.com/Rizzoli